2020 THE END OF THE BEGINNING

Continuing the eternal journey

DAVID SHAW

Also from this author:

An Average Joe's Search for the Meaning of Life.

New Mediumship: the spiritual
transcripts of an Average Joe.

Ghost Writers.

2020 The End of the Beginning
ISBN: 9798697798904

CONTENTS

ACKNOWLEDGEMENTS

I would like to first and foremost thank my family for supporting the writing of this book throughout the last five years. It has been a marathon at times and I know that I haven't always been the most 'switched on' individual when writing in a trance mode!

I would also like to thank everybody that has joined me in a spiritual vocation during this period, in whatever capacity – sorry there are too many people to mention individually, but you have all made my work just that little bit easier.

Thank you to my spirit team for supporting and advising on every subject covered in the book. Special thanks must go to the wise old man – this book could not have been written without all of your input. I am forever and sincerely just your messenger.

Finally, thanks to you, the reader of this book. I know that many of you will have lost someone close to you as a result of the virus and my heart really does go out to you. Their lives were not lost in vain; I can wholeheartedly promise you that. I can also promise you that they will be by your side as you read every word that's been written, since this book belongs to them every bit as much as it belongs to you. Life goes on in all dimensions – why wouldn't it?

The year 2020 shall all but introduce the end of the beginning. We are the future… and that future is now.

This book is dedicated to everyone and anyone
who ever graced this wondrous life.

INTRODUCTION

In the five years that it has taken to complete this book, there have been three different titles; two complete rewrites, and a whole new spirit team joining the writers club - the reasons for which I will explain.

On reflection, much has happened in our world over these last five years and I'm afraid that there is inevitably a lot more to come very soon that will test our resolve beyond anything that's ever come before.

Two thirds of this book was written before the beginning of 2020; before yours truly hit 'writers block'. I couldn't understand why I was struggling to connect to my spirit friends and instigate the completion of the book. It was as if they had slammed on the brakes just before I hit an almighty brick wall.

In many ways, since January 2020, a procession of brick walls have been placed in front of us and many more will continue to appear for a long time yet.

This five year project began with a view to assist the people of this world to do a little bit of soul-searching that would make their transition to the spirit dimension just that little bit easier. Alas, circumstances have now changed somewhat and that task has become considerably more difficult.

Nevertheless, the guidelines remain the same. Everything that we do or encounter should always be classed as experiences – good or bad in perception. What lies ahead for us in the spirit dimension will be dependent on how we react to each and every experience and whether we can accept life in every form that it comes in.

In essence, many of us will have been here before in another guise. This is our moment to finally break free from the fetters of time; from the manacles of self-doubt, and the shackles of guilty consequences.

I have been aware for quite some time what lies ahead after the impact of the Covid-19 virus has affected society. Furthermore, I now know how long it will be before the world returns to a relative normality. I strongly advise that you read the entire book before finding out for yourself. Believe in yourself and nothing will ever deter you from a rewarding life.

This book is a detailed account of the next step in my own eternal journey, just seven years after initially searching for the true meaning of life. In so many ways, it may also be a version of your own perpetual voyage.

For all of us, let us now look forward to the end of our beginning…

As always, any text written in an italic format has been delivered directly from spirit guides and has not been edited in any shape or form.

CHAPTER 1
A Spiritual Passport

From a scientific perspective, the word 'life' often refers to anything and everything that has the ability to metabolise and grow, whether it be stationed at the bottom of the deepest ocean, or marooned on a distant Galaxy that's still to be discovered. Our vast Universe is shared by more life forms than we could ever mathematically compute and every single one of them is considered unique in their own specific way, either through physical appearance or conceptual functionality. Even so, a communal bonding must forever remain in place, linking every conceivable life force in its collective slipstream. That special bonding is the kernel of all that is deemed to be 'spirit'.

Life on Earth could be compared to an enormous food buffet where you can eat as much as you like, with the option to keep returning for more. There are no limitations to what's on offer and the only set rule is that you continually progress from every single visit.

To all intents and purposes, this is the basis for all that is considered 'life', whether it be the breath that carries you home, the ghost that reminds you of eternal existence, or the consciousness that fuels endless journeys.

Life on Earth is fundamentally simplistic – it is only human nature that chooses to complicate it. Yet, through all the trials and tribulations that are continually thrown our way, there is surely an aspect of beauty in every moment of breath that greets us. It is this inherent splendour that allures us to Earth in the first place, before our impending voyage home to our next life in the spirit world gives us the opportunity to reflect on all that we have learned through our experiences.

Logistically, any journey of this magnitude will require a valid passport, but this passport cannot be bought with money – it must be earned through spiritual endeavours. Then, once this spiritual passport is authenticated, the gates to the soul will truly open - and endless voyages will really begin to evolve.

The spirit dimension, in many facets, is entirely different from the material world that we presently reside in. It is inhabited entirely from pure consciousness and everything that may appear material to us is in fact processed through pure thought. When we dream or meditate in our present physical existence, we momentarily enter this non-materialistic environment and any subsequent communication received from spirit people is entirely symbolic. Therefore, we should understand that a spiritual passport can only ever exist in our mind, yet its importance should never be underestimated.

If we are to return to the spirit dimension as a more knowledgeable and more evolved individual then we must have accomplished each task that was initially set out for us before we arrived on the Earth plane. However, the great challenge of living a physical life, where our physical senses are normally at the forefront of our existence, is that in this dimension we are, for the most part, blissfully unaware of just what these tasks actually are.

So how exactly do we find out what these tasks entail? And furthermore, how do we know if we have achieved the desired outcome? The honest answer is that you won't truly know until you return to the spirit dimension, and only then will you discover whether your life on Earth has been as successful as you would have hoped.

To further complicate this matter, we are all at different stages of ascension in the spiritual ladder, so what may be important to your own personal spiritual progression might be completely different to your wife or husband, or anybody else that you know. In fact, it is highly unlikely that you will have the same spiritual goals as anybody else on Earth. The reason for this declaration is actually quite logical.

When we return to the spirit dimension we are judged on our compassionate achievements; on how we rose to the challenges set out for us, and how we emotionally coped with any disappointments. This all sounds fairly straightforward, but the truth is that the individual tasked with judging all of our achievements and disenchantments will always be the harshest critic;

the most ruthless adjudicator, and will almost certainly be the most demanding person to please that you will ever encounter. That person is 'you', so as you can now appreciate, the goals set out for us are as individual as we are to each other.

The function of 'time' has no representation whatsoever in the spirit dimension. This means that anything and everything that you act upon will always seem instantaneous. There is no physical matter to slow things down – everything is totally controlled by our thoughts. In the spirit dimension, where consciousness cannot be burdened by onerous physical senses, your thoughts can become the most powerful force imaginable – nothing can slow thoughts down or get in their way – apart from maybe your consciousness itself! How many times have you thought about faraway places in your dreams, only to be instantly transported there? This is more or less how we function in the spirit dimension and the possibilities are endless.

When we do eventually find ourselves back in the spirit dimension, we are given the job of reviewing our life just passed in the physical world. Every single thought and action that previously manifested through our physical existence is subsequently analysed in order to ascertain if we achieved our goals. Thankfully, this mammoth task is much more easily accomplished in the spirit dimension as our speed of thought is vastly improved and as we have just mentioned – time does not exist here and cannot interfere with the workings of our highly evolving consciousness.

Nevertheless, the job of reviewing our recently ended physical incarnation is still an extremely arduous one. In the spirit dimension there are no egotistical or materialistic values present within this environment, meaning that we cannot judge ourselves through self-ordained merits or self-indulgent privileges that would otherwise have been prominent in a corporeal society. Here, the intrinsic values are based on pure logic. For example, if an individual was rewarded financially for a particular achievement in a life just passed then this would bear little merit in a non-materialistic culture.

Every single one of us will have our spiritual passport on hand when we return to the spirit dimension. Therefore, our task is a fairly straightforward one - to get this passport authenticated, which will then allow us to continue with this great adventure.

I'm now going to let you in on a little secret… there are ways of getting our passport authenticated without knowing exactly what each of our particular tasks are, even though these tasks are completely individual to us. We must remember that we are the souls charged with deciding whether or not our life in the physical world was a just and worthy one. And if we can somehow become aware of what values and principles are important once we return to the spirit world, then it's fair to say that each and every one of our goals will fall within these ethics, thus allowing us to be much better prepared for our final assessment.

So with this philosophy in mind, I would now like you to imagine that you are standing at the customs desk, passport in hand, duty-free stuffed safely away, and about to be grilled about your holiday just ended. Suddenly, you catch the eye of the customs officer who looks at you pensively before summoning you forward. Instinctively, you look down at your passport and find a checklist of guidelines that require your attention. Everything on this list must be ticked before the large box at the bottom of the passport can have any chance of being stamped with your own personal approval.

This is your opportunity to be prepared for whatever lies ahead in the spirit dimension. The next ten chapters will be your guidelines as to whether your soul is ready to accept the challenge of eternal living.

The list is as follows:

- My life is far from perfect.
- I am willing to forgive myself as well as others.
- My heart skips a beat at the end of "It's a Wonderful Life."
- The only wealth that I truly need is knowledge.
- Every soul has the ability to share love.
- I am the creator of all that is truthful.
- I am willing to accept any failures as a success.
- I am no more impressive than the humblest of hobos.
- I must heal myself before attempting to heal others.
- I am but one small part of the evolution of eternal life

You must remember that these are only guidelines and there may be instances where a more thorough review is required. Nevertheless, if you can acknowledge the ethics instilled within each chapter then you will be in a far better position to begin the next exciting chapter in your eternal life.

Your destiny now awaits you. You may begin…

CHAPTER 2
My Life is Far from Perfect

The time is 7pm, perhaps my favourite time of the day. This is the time when most of the people in the town of Irvine start to relax and unwind after a typically stressful day. It's the middle of January and the climate is so stereotypical of a Scottish winter – cold, damp and excruciatingly miserable – just the type of weather that the people of this small Ayrshire town have come to expect.

Yet, despite the unappealing conditions, the view from the thirteenth floor of this high-rise building is simply breath-taking, and looking out from the rooftop I feel as if I'm on top of the world as street lights adorn the horizon for as far as my appreciative eyes can see, bringing depth to the landscape in a way that only an artist could surely replicate. Occasionally, a splattering of traffic interrupts this majestic portrait in a collage of movement, shape-shifting succinctly between streets too dark to matter. When suddenly, a shadow appears in a window, silhouetted by the moonlight, and I am reminded of what makes this masterpiece so special, yet so overwhelmingly difficult to comprehend, since I instantly realise that the beauty of this moment is surreal, that it can never be complete without true substance and real meaning.

Legend suggests that behind every window a winter's tale is gradually being written, where every story is no less important than the first story ever told. Therefore, if I am to truly enjoy this moment, this period of absolute tranquillity, I must first acknowledge that we cannot truly view life by what is solely perceived in our own mind, since life can be as cruel as the darkened window that hides it, yet as splendid as the brightness that fashions it.

Life may brave a breath in your town and in my town; from the rooftop of this tall building to the parapet of your compact family nest; sometimes creating havoc in its seductive slipstream, otherwise just drifting along in a mirage of colours, engulfing all in its wake, whilst onlookers admire the subtleness of its inner beauty.

Life is but the path created by the mind; the journey endured by the body; the 'joie de vivre' fashioned by the soul. But what is life but an empty vessel; bereft of substance without a cargo in tow; set adrift on repatriated waters, a purpose to neither seek nor validate? What is life without fuel to neither reason nor determine, if only to harbour a surreal nothingness, stifled by causeless ideals?

Now, as more and more lights disappear from this fading Scottish skyline, it is difficult not to feel alone. Sometimes life can be the loneliest companion to even the most vivacious traveller. Yet, as I now gaze out of my own personal window, I instantly realise that I have never felt more alive.

If an artist painted a picture of the perfect life, what would the visual features consist of? Would the subject of the painting be human, animal, or just some abstract symbol that contained a unique reference of beauty that only the creator of this masterpiece could truly understand? Perhaps a glimpse of the perfect life is only ever visible through the eyes of every individual artist, since beauty is, as they so often say, in the eyes of the beholder.

Vincent Van Gogh was an artist who, by his own admission, lived a life that was far from perfect. His incessant drive towards global recognition as a classic artist invariably drove him to the brink of insanity. His well-publicised self-mutilation created a notoriety that drew derision from his fellow artists, before he eventually ended his life in a passionless manner. Ironically, his work became far more popular after his death; indeed his paintings are now considered more valuable than the wealth of some small countries. In retrospect, we can now ascertain that Van Gogh is one of the most famous artists that ever painted, and if he were alive today then surely his iconic success would've prevented him from physically and mentally destroying himself.

But, on the other hand, what if it was his mental torture that helped to create his masterpieces? What if his relentless struggle for recognition helped to generate a passion in his work that could not have been replicated in a more relaxed and stable mind? What if a life that has been deemed to be truly awful could create paintings that signify perfection in the eyes of millions of critics? What then does that say about a man who could feel so alone inside, yet still produce images of beauty that have brought so much joy and pleasure to millions of souls still searching for their own perfect life?

If Van Gogh currently resides in the spirit world then we cannot be certain if he appreciates this new found popularity of his work, since the underlying effects of materialism will no longer be of any great significance to his conscious development. Nevertheless, if his previously tortured persona is still actively searching for some magical inner beauty then the legacy that he has left behind on Earth shall surely instil warmth deep within his eternal soul.

I have often been referred to as a highly spiritual individual by the readers of my books. In fact, many readers have often sought out my advice on how to improve their lives, which always leaves me with a bit of a dilemma. On the one hand, I want to help or advise them in any way that I can, yet on the other hand I must be as open and honest as possible with any advice that I relay.

The truth is that I am no more of a spiritual being than the person who seeks my advice. You may think that I present the information for this publication with a certain sense of opulence, but these words have been borne through countless mistakes and imperfections. In fact, I have just rewritten this entire paragraph several times since it has been littered with errors – and probably still isn't perfect! But that's why I must write this book - to be able to make countless grammatical errors; to continually learn from every single mistake; to realise that it's all my imperfections that have moulded the person I have become, and to understand that sometimes life needs to be dragged through the gutter before it's recuperated through justifiable ideals that forever remind us of our impunities. Therefore, for me to pronounce a life of utter perfection at the time of my return to the spirit world would be a declaration as fallacious as the misguided notion that success is purely based on material wealth.

Life is but an energy-based consciousness that can never die and continually evolves. As you read each word in this book, your consciousness automatically consumes this information and assimilates its content appropriately. Subsequently, if the information is then interpreted as detrimental to the overall ethical stature of the consciousness, then there is a strong possibility that the physical body may be affected in some way. Fears and emotions are a mainstay of our everyday lives on Earth and as such control most of our physical actions and endeavours. Learning to live with this inherent lifestyle is part of our conditioning as emotive individuals.

Therefore, if life is truly eternal and we do eventually evolve through physical death into a lifeform based purely on conscious thinking, then we must presume that, without the fear and pain associated with the physical world, life in the next dimension will be much more beneficial to our welfare. In fact, it sounds absolutely perfect, doesn't it? Of course it does, but if that was the case then why do many of us choose to return to Earth and face such a traumatic life once more?

The physical world that we presently live in is filled with continuous personal challenges; some are easily dealt with, whilst others may tear us to shreds with torment. Success in this lifetime is often misconstrued as a competition to attain material domination over others. Indeed, a life where every conceivable luxury item can be obtained by simply snapping one's fingers may appear to bring perfection in many people's eyes.

Conversely, the sudden realisation that excessive personal wealth cannot always guarantee a pain-free, uber-healthy lifestyle can make even the most self-obsessed individual realise that life on Earth will always be at the mercy of a constantly decaying natural habitat.

With that analogy in mind, it is important that we now begin to understand the main differentials between the morals and principles with which we try to instil in our present physical life, and the ethical values that govern our consciousness in the afterlife. To achieve this, we must first look within ourselves and find what's really important to us in all aspects of benevolent living.

We are taught from an early age that law, order and governance are the archetypal doctrines required for maintaining a thriving society. Add in some additional ingredients here and there, such as religion, marriage, 2.2 children and a three-bed-semi in suburbia, and you have what many pragmatists would claim to be a perfect life. And what's wrong with that, you may very well ask? To be fair – not a lot, especially if this particular life format exudes compassion and kinship throughout its overlying boundaries.

However, nobody has ever arrived on this Earth plane with the sole objective of finding a perfect life. Such a task is simply not possible in a lifetime that is endless and forever changing. The reality is that we have arrived here to experience life in its most challenging format, where the self-induced illusion of death eagerly awaits us – challenging our beliefs and ideals until it strikes us directly. We may contemplate returning to Earth with the knowledge that consciousness survives after the physical body dies but the emotional distress created through bereavement will still affect us with a devastating force.

Likewise, disease and serious illness can be a relentless enemy, testing our resolve to its extreme limits, and death is often the only solution to such an overwhelmingly unpleasant experience. So the question becomes even more intriguing – why put ourselves through such a distressing state of mind, knowing that watching a loved one in pain is so upsetting? Is life so precious that we must always endure so many hardships? The answer will always be 'yes', since we can never fully understand the true essence of compassionate love until we have at least tasted the bitterness of sorrow that yields it.

If you were to consider the nature of the spirit dimension and its timeless variables then such an existence within this domain might seem like an eternity – never-ending and indefinite. Indeed, any opportunity to be able to escape from this endless timeframe and journey back to the transitory material world would be appealing to any individual, regardless of the associated emotional baggage that always accompanies such a trip. It is also fair to say that if you considered any impending return to the physical world then the thought of enduring physical death or even terminal illness wouldn't necessarily affect your judgement too much since you already know that life must continue afterwards. Suffice to say, a journey back to the Earth plane from the spirit world would be an adventure worthy of any weary traveller, such is the vast range of experiences and knowledge that would be gained throughout the short stay. In fact, it might just feel like taking a year out from your studies – perhaps a 'Gap Year', which would allow you to travel to new places and experience life as you have never known it – warts and all, before returning back to the spirit dimension to utilise all that you have learned from your experiences, and to share them with other likeminded people.

Gap Years are often regarded as one of the best times of any young adult's life on Earth. This sudden freedom to roam wherever you desire, meet people of the same mind-set, discover new cultures, become completely self-dependant, and perhaps even fall in love for the first time – are all life changing experiences that can help an individual to fully appreciate the precious gift that they have been given. The memories of which are often stored in video recordings or photographs, to be perused in later life, once a more conformist or predictable family life ensues.

Nowadays, many mature adults are also choosing to take a Gap Year away from the pressures of their stressful day-to-day job. Indeed, modern day employment benefits now make it possible for some people to just up-sticks and leave everything behind for a while, in order to rejuvenate one's soul in places where life is much more slow-paced or perhaps down to earth. The point being that in the physical world, age is no longer the barrier that it may previously have been, proving that you are never too young or old to really start living again, or to simply rediscover yourself.

A few years ago, one of my closest friends became totally disillusioned with his job and decided to take a Gap Year, with a view to travelling the world on his own. He was in his thirties and had very little previous experience of travelling on his own, yet he found himself visiting places that you wouldn't normally associate with tourism. He travelled from Romania to Siberia, then as far east as Iran and Palestine. When he later arrived in a small village in Cambodia, he was astounded to learn that he was in fact the first European that the locals had ever seen. Finally, he was given the rare opportunity to visit the most secretive country in the world – a place where even Kings, Queens, Presidents and Prime Ministers wouldn't necessarily be allowed in. This was a place so enigmatic that very little has ever been known about the people who live there. My friend would later recall his account of North Korea as grim and disturbing, yet totally fascinating.

When he eventually returned from his travels he was continually asked why he chose to visit places like Iran and North Korea. He would answer, "Because they're different from anything that I have ever been used to." He would add that on his travels he met some wonderful people, regardless of their beliefs or material status. His everlasting memory was of the gracious courtesy he was shown by people everywhere, and the fact that they were always willing to welcome him into their world for as long as he wished to stay.

I have always been envious of my friend's incredible trip. Listening to his fascinating tales of how life is so different on the other side of the world often makes me wish that I had the courage to replicate his path and discover for myself how diverse life on Earth really is. In retrospect, we can always listen intently to the captivating account of those who have chosen to venture into these unknown lands or we can simply read books about faraway shores where everything may seem completely alien to our regimented lifestyle, but unless you have actually been to these places then you can never truly appreciate the nature of the experience on a personal basis.

Likewise, in the spirit dimension we are taught about living with a physical body and the emotions that accompany such an existence. We may obliquely understand the theory behind physicality but we can never truly appreciate its principles and dynamics unless we first-hand choose to endorse a life processed in this way. Choosing to return to Earth is no different from entering places like North Korea or Cambodia, or anywhere else that presents a new expanse for us to explore. Hence, when we return from our travels, we can share our experience with others, before they too have the opportunity to follow in our footsteps.

Of course, not everyone who begins a Gap Year manages to finish the full term. For some, the decision to deliberately end their trip can come at a great price and will often be tarnished with regrets. Sometimes the time spent away brings an emotional response that is just too much to bear. Every journey is different to each individual and can only ever be judged as such. It is a prerequisite that each trip always begins and ends at the bequest of any soul's intention. Even so, any decision to terminate this journey should never be taken lightly as the overall objectives are unlikely to be completed.

In all my years of performing mediusmship I have never yet communicated with someone who has no regrets from prematurely ending their physical life. The underlying emotional problems that caused such an act will still lie at the forefront of their consciousness after physical death. The only solace available being a further opportunity to recommence another Gap Year and thus face those demons head on once again. As always, there are no direct lessons to be learned from ending one's time on Earth – lessons can only ever be learned from living. Thankfully, the beauty of eternal life ensures that there will always be opportunities to educate ourselves further in whatever capacity we so choose.

The flip side of the coin is that some people will return home early from their Gap Year through no fault of their own. Natural death at a young age in the physical world will always seem unfair and undeserving, yet the reality is that when a soul returns to the spirit dimension then they will personally judge themselves on how well they lived, rather than how long. In actual fact, it is possible to take just one solitary breath and fulfil your purpose here on Earth, whilst at the same time you could live for over a hundred years and still not come close to achieving a desired outcome.

There are infinite reasons as to why anyone should return to Earth on their very own personal Gap Year. But, never has anyone set out with the expectation of finding a perfect life. Such a proclamation would be deemed ridiculous in the spirit dimension, where an entire Universe that is constantly changing, is continually open for exploration.

Perhaps what we really intend to look for when setting foot on this planet is a chance to re-examine all of our previous imperfections from earlier Gap Years. We can only wonder if Vincent Van Gogh would choose to act any differently should he return to Earth, since he should now be well aware of the fact that success in the physical domain is not based on how much money his paintings command at auction, but rather how a creative mind can educate others as well as ourselves.

And now, as I pensively gaze out over this hazy Ayrshire skyline, my thoughts drift like the tide, wondering if my own imperfections will raise my conscious awareness sufficiently so that every remaining word in this book does justice to the people of this small Scottish town, as well as the billions of souls still searching for a meaning to their life.

CHAPTER 3

I am willing to forgive myself as well as others

There is no doubt that the act of forgiving someone is a prerequisite for effectively ascending to the spirit dimension from the remnants of any physical existence. But forgiving someone else will always seem like a walk in the park compared to attempting to forgive one's self, and the information that I will now bring forward may totally change your perception on life. I know that it changed my own understanding of why life may seem so overwhelmingly cruel to some, yet so easy-going for others.

Philosopher and businessman, Paul Boese, famously quoted that "Forgiveness does not change the past, but it does enlarge the future." The use of the word 'enlarge' is what makes this particular statement both interesting and intriguing. Fundamentally, this statement suggests that if we cannot forgive someone then our lives will be ring-fenced within self-induced boundaries, unable to break free from loveless constraints. In the physical world that we know, any personal act of forgiving can often feel like a great weight has suddenly been lifted from our shoulders, often resulting in a more positive outlook for both forgiver and the person being forgiven. Indeed, the sudden urge to forgive someone will essentially release the shackles that were previously holding you back, thus allowing the freedom to start truly living again.

In the physical world, where both emotional and physical pain is a vital part of learning, there are certain aspects of human behaviour that will understandably be extremely difficult to forgive. For example, how can you possibly forgive someone who has intentionally ended the life of a member of your family? The simple answer is that you almost certainly can't. Our natural perception of life on Earth is that it's too precious to be terminated by someone else. To do so might seem as if you had forgotten all about the pain and distress that had been caused by the perpetrator of such a callous act. It is fair to say that subsequent life on Earth for anyone who has suffered such a horrendous fate will never seem the same again, and will often be tarred by negative emotions - such as anger and sorrow.

Consequently, would this inability to forgive someone for such a crime now deter an individual from entering the spirit world? Would a spiritual passport be refused if someone still harboured a grudge against a killer? The answer is mainly dependent on whether we are now prepared to look at life from a different angle. We have already discussed the fact that nobody can ever return to the spirit dimension after having attained a life of perfection. Now we must decide if any actions undertaken on the physical domain can be justified, and if we can learn from the repercussions of these choices in order to enlarge our future existence within the spirit realms.

Throughout the history of time on Earth, humans have been inflicting incalculable extents of suffering on each other, from barbaric ancient times when survival often consisted of maliciously killing whoever disagreed with your blinkered viewpoint, to the modern day annihilation of ethnic minorities in countries where dignified constitutions have capitulated.

The consensus of opinion must surely be that humans will never learn how to live in harmony in the same way that spirit people do. However, if we truly are on this physical planet to learn about the physicality of life; to experience the emotional pain that accompanies violence and abuse; to witness the hugely immoral admiration and endorsement of prejudicial views, and to discover that fear and loathing are predominant parts of human survival, then perhaps we should begin to understand that the darker side of human nature will always be evident in everything that surrounds us. But, for every dark side to our existence, there is always a greater good, a warmer embrace, a firmer handshake, and a breath of fresh air where staleness once prevailed. Only an act of forgiveness can effectively instil these wonderful qualities once a soul understands and accepts the consequences of their immoral actions and thoughts.

There is no doubt that when we return to the spirit dimension our perception of life alters to suit the environment. No longer will we have to fear death or its consequences since there clearly is no physical decay to our soul, nor is there any need to protect ourselves from the wrath of nature – which will now compliment us rather than fight against us.

When we initially return to the spirit world we quickly realise that whatever happened in the physical life that's just ended does not affect us with the same force as it did before. For example, if we arrived back in the spirit world after having been murdered then the sudden realisation that life has not ended indefinitely will almost certainly make the task of forgiving our killer that much easier. It will still be our choice as to whether we do forgive each act of cruelty previously inflicted upon ourselves or our loved-one's, but we will be shown by our new tutors that progress in the spirit realm is dependent on whether we can accept that each of us is at a different stage of learning, and that you cannot learn how to truly appreciate the joy of eternal living unless you have first experienced the pain of believing that it has been taken from you.

I'm fairly sure that the idea of forgiving a killer will seem totally crass to many readers. However, in the spirit world the only judge and jury will always be you, and once you are shown just how much pain and sorrow most murderers suffer when they return to the spirit world then the task becomes just that little bit easier.

As a past-life therapist, I have hypnotised many people and subsequently been privy to some incredible accounts of crimes being committed against my clients. The world was certainly a far more barbaric place centuries ago, when law and order was nowhere near as articulate as it is today. In my own experience, I have also been regressed to lives that were prematurely ended by homicide upon my person – from being speared by a Roman soldier; to being brutally stabbed through the heart during the Jacobean era, all of which were deeply unpleasant and left me feeling rather disconcerted afterwards. But, by far my most unpleasant experience of regression was when I found myself in a past life as the murderer, rather than as the victim.

This awful existence as a viscous killer in 19th century Australia has been well documented elsewhere in my previous books and as such has left an indelible stain on my character - and one that I am still deeply ashamed of. My reluctance to write about this life in any great detail is based on the fact that I was deeply traumatised after the whole experience. The feelings of shame and torment that affected me immediately after the regressions were extremely difficult to bear and my conscious decision to never again be regressed was not taken lightly. Nevertheless, we have already established that life is just an endless list of experiences that we must learn from and I do believe that my current physical life has proven to me that I have since developed a strong respect for all living creatures.

Forgiving yourself after such a horrendous catalogue of crimes will always be extremely difficult once returning to the spirit dimension. The key is being able to accept what has transpired rather than purely atoning for any misdemeanours. There is no doubt that accepting the fact that you ended the lives of others will always be far more difficult to comprehend than accepting any admission of guilt from those who ended your own life. As I have previously stated, in the spirit dimension there is no need to judge others for their actions – you only judge yourself.

In the physical world that we live in, the media constantly reminds us of unsolved murders. This must be excruciatingly distressing for any soul directly affected by such a nightmare, since the feeling that someone has been allowed to get away with this most heinous of crimes will relentlessly tear at their broken heart. To live with the knowledge that a loved one has perished at the hands of a murderer who has evaded justice will always be one of the greatest tests of anyone's will.

However, when you return to the spirit world you will find that there is no hiding place for any murderer; there is no jury prepared to consider your leniency, and there is no greater judge on your character than the person who suddenly realises the inglorious effect that their immoral actions have had on another soul. Such a sudden and chilling realisation is a million times more punishing than any prison sentence could ever be. In essence - forgiving yourself will always be far more difficult than forgiving others.

I sincerely hope that this information will comfort anyone in this world who believes that justice has let them down. From my own personal experience – there is absolutely no escape from your own self. In the spirit world there is only consciousness – and your own conscience must always be clear before you can finally start to appreciate true love. Anything else is but an experience.

> *"Only when souls have rid themselves of all personal regrets, can they accept and understand the regrets of others. Only when souls can forgive themselves, can they begin to forgive others. Only when souls effectively return to the spirit world, can life be enlarged in a world blessed with forgiveness and compassion."*
>
> Chung.

CHAPTER 4

My heart skips a beat at the end of the film 'It's a Wonderful Life'

The iconic Christmas movie, 'It's a Wonderful life', is still regularly broadcast around the world every single year; the film's timeless morals reminding every viewer that Christmas is an iconic period when the power of love should be much more appealing than the power of a bulging purse full of dollars.

At the end of the film, our fallen hero, George, is saved from a life of financial ruin by his fellow man, woman, and guardian angel – and not surprisingly, everyone then lives happily ever after. The underlying message being, of course, that materialism in any shape or form is not necessarily beneficial to anyone's long standing future in this lifetime.

But it's not essentially the fact that George is eventually recompensed for his financial shortfall that makes many a heart suddenly skip a beat, nor is it the fact that George decides not to jump off the bridge in order to save the reputation of his family – it's more the fact that every one of George's friends decide to rally round to help him when he really needs it most, despite the fact that he had inadvertently lost all of their savings.

Throughout the film, we can see how George is a good man. His life is predominantly centred on helping his community and making sure his family is well provided for. At times, you could be forgiven for believing that George lived the perfect life as he was well respected in every sense of the word; he was the sort of father that every man hopes to be; the type of husband that every wife hopes to find, and that special kind of soul that every angel would want to guide. Yet, as we invariably find out, a life blessed in this perceivably flawless fashion is ultimately found to be less than perfect. For as we have already established – perfection is just a dream that you will always wake up from.

Critics argue that this film highlights all that is good about human nature, yet society still encourages us to spend, spend, spend in a materialistic avalanche of yuletide extravagance, in the hope that our loved-one's will appreciate us more than they already do. The pretence being that Christmas is the one time of the year when we are allowed to go just a little overboard on personal expenditure, even though the consequence of such reckless behaviour may cause the best of us to end up like poor old George.

However, it could also be argued that whenever a family member finds themselves in a similar crisis, then the strength and willpower of the family as a whole will surely overcome all obstacles, thus creating a much stronger social bond than before. The very same principles can be applied when close friends support each other. In times of need, the human spirit will always be lifted by the collective love of kindred spirits.

One of the most testing times for any human being is attending the funeral of a loved-one. The debilitating properties of sudden bereavement will usually have a profoundly upsetting effect on even the most heartless of individuals and the prospect of enduring such an event is often too much to bear. Nevertheless, most of us still choose to attend the funeral and pay our respects, after somehow finding the strength and willpower to face this emotional pain head on.

When attending funerals, I have often wondered why I am not aware of any spirit people desperately trying to contact me. After all, there is a room full of people in need of comforting due to a somewhat misguided belief that those who die will never be seen or heard of again. Wouldn't the person who has just passed over want me to relay the fact that they are still alive and aware of everything that is happening around them? Wouldn't they want me to help their friends and family to understand that life must continue despite what has recently happened? Logic would suggest that spirit mediums would be the ideal people to conduct and facilitate funerals, since we have the ability to suggest that there is no death; that life is continual and we should all celebrate this fact, instead of mourning the loss of someone who has simply moved on to the next stage of their life development. But, life on Earth doesn't quite work like that, does it? In retrospect, we are all here to experience physical life and death, and if that means experiencing the emotional pain that accompanies physical death then naturally that is what we must endure in order to appreciate true love in all of its capacities.

In truth, no ethical spirit medium would ever choose to deliver a message to someone at a funeral. It's simply not the time and place to offer this form of healing, no matter the circumstances. Mediums, like any other people at funerals, are better placed just offering support through empathy. Sometimes, just offering someone a shoulder to cry on can lift a soul through the darkest of periods, knowing that their pain is shared and understood.

I find it utterly amazing how people somehow find the strength to get through such a horrendous experience. For me, it is truly enlightening to know that when we are at our most vulnerable then the support of family and friends, in both the physical and spirit domains, will always lift us through the worst of times. This is the phenomenal power of the collective consciousness – a partnership between great minds in the physical and spirit dimensions, both working in harmony to support souls in need of healing – just as they helped George at the conclusion of the film.

In this predominantly physical world, the popular definition of a 'family' is a group of people united by certain convictions or a common affiliation. In other words, a family is a social pact that is either formed through choice or derived from appropriation. Either way, this collective assembly of entities is what many spiritual philosophers often regard as *soul groups*. Soul groups are powerful unions that offer protection and security from emotional turmoil and heartache. The closeness of this social bond is highlighted by the fact that if just one member of the group should become emotionally distressed then each and every other member shall also endure a similar experience, regardless of any personal circumstances.

Having to endure the physical death of a child is easily the most harrowing experience that any parent will ever have to undergo and will test human nature to its extreme limits. Likewise, should a family be torn apart by events determined by war, crime, deception or even a simple misunderstanding that cannot be put right, then the core of the soul group is often stretched beyond the limit of our understanding – but, the seal can never be broken, regardless of the underlying circumstances.

Sometimes, we just need to open up our mind to the notion that somewhere in our soul there is a piece of music that defines who we are. This wondrous sound can only ever be heard by the members of our soul group as its annotations reverb around our hearts, reminding us of the power of unity, the strength of creativity, and the values of compassion.

"And sometimes, we just need to listen to the song in our heart as it seeks out long lost friends; rekindles old flames, and regains someone's trust. The beauty of this song is that it reminds us of a once-forgotten world, where harmony was in abundance, and where love was all that ever really mattered."

"And sometimes, we fight battles that can never be won; we love people that refuse to be loved; we cry tears that can never run dry; we punish others instead of ourselves; we seek vengeance from compassionate Gods, and we run from the truth - when the truth seems more terrifying than any lie."

"And sometimes, our heart will skip a beat when we least expect it. And when it does, the heart of every member of our soul group will do likewise, whether it's in this physical existence or in a once-forgotten world that's waiting patiently for our safe return."

George's life may not have been perfect, but it could easily be regarded as 'wonderful' in constitution. After all, his soul group successfully lifted him from the depths of despair with a gentle but firm reminder that strength in kinship is far more enriching than the forte of singularity. Naturally, what we always discover throughout our time here on Earth is that fear will adversely affect the individual far more than the cluster, and there won't always be a safety-net for individuals who find themselves being persecuted through no fault of their own, since sometimes every turn in the road must be negotiated before you find the best way home. Only when an individual eventually realises that life is merely an emotional experience and not a continuous battle against uncertainties, can they appreciate the beauty and wonder of a collective consciousness of souls. For many, this won't become apparent until they return to the spirit dimension, where persistent fears can be removed indefinitely.

One of my favourite spiritual vocations is participating in deep trance mediumship. This purposeful endeavour allows me to be educated in the different facets of eternal life-forces. The spirit people who are channelled during trance mediumship have a far greater knowledge of everything that exists beyond our scope of reasoning and the ability to receive information from this source permits a much greater understanding of why life experiences on this planet are so important to our overall educational structure.

A question that's regularly asked in these sessions is 'Why are people in third world countries continually starving to death whilst those of us on this side of the globe enjoy an excess of natural resources?' The answer consistently brought forward from various spirit guides is usually received with great surprise, although in rational terms makes perfect sense. I would now like to expand on this answer in greater detail.

Let's say, for example, that you are a news reporter and you are presenting a report on a terrible famine that is claiming millions of lives in an African country. The extent of such a report will almost certainly have a deeply upsetting effect on you. However, as the famine does not directly affect your current way of life, you will almost certainly continue with a fruitful lifestyle that is devoid of the horrors that are devastating people fighting the famine. But, if you were then sent to this country to report directly from the source of the problem; witnessing children dying from hunger through helpless eyes of sorrow, then the turmoil of such a harrowing experience would surely instigate within you a far deeper sense of pain. It is indeed one thing to read or hear about such a horror, but it is entirely different to experience it first-hand. A disturbing experience such as this will almost certainly remain with you long after you return to your present way of life, and may have a long-lasting effect on your way of appreciating life.

Our understanding of any particular way of life is far greater when we actually witness it occurring, rather than read about it through reports written by others. We may not have the ability to personally alter this devastation but we can actively encourage others to visit this place and try to better understand the values associated with human life. Then, we can share what we have learned, with a hope that it makes us more appreciative of the little things in life – like waking up in the morning and not having to worry about where your family is going to find enough food to eat. And... we can also learn about the big things in life – like discovering that your loved-one has been taken from this life, yet the love you have for them can never die... and will only ever grow stronger, even through immense heartache, no matter the circumstances of their passing.

Through trance mediumship, I have been reliably informed that every single soul that incarnates to Earth is given a preview of how their life will unfold in great detail. This is a privilege that is afforded to us before we accept the challenge of improving our knowledge of physical living and the emotions that accompany such a task. Therefore, we can then deduce that every single soul that dies from hunger on Earth will have agreed beforehand to set foot on this world despite the lifestyle that surely awaits them.

To try and understand this from our own physical perspective will probably seem extremely crass. However, when you embark on such a journey from the spirit dimension, where eternal life is understood, then any impending life on Earth is only ever a short-term opportunity to improve one's knowledge, before returning to share our experiences – just like the news reporter. Then, once this knowledge is shared appropriately, others will follow in our spiritual footsteps, and the great cycle of knowledge will continue to educate us on the fact that the love shared between souls is always more enriching than anything that the natural world throws at us.

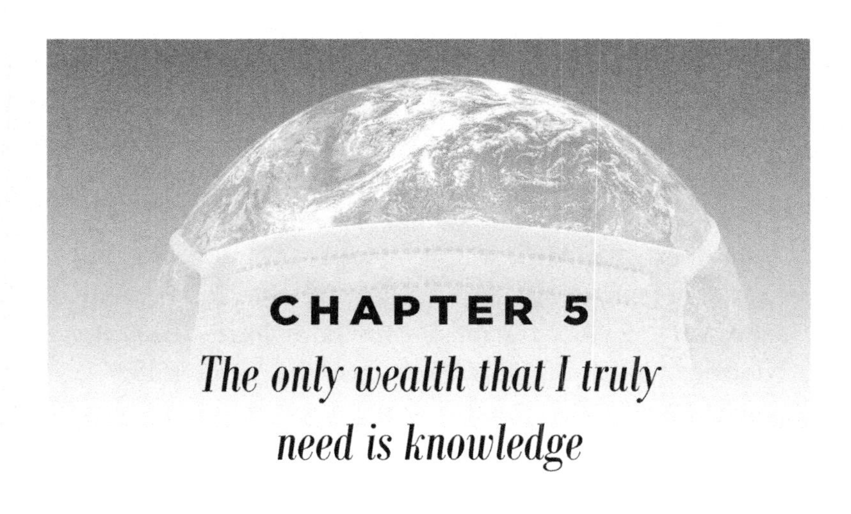

CHAPTER 5
The only wealth that I truly need is knowledge

Knowledge has been the mainstay of all perpetual living throughout the history of being, resulting in a hypothesis that suggests – to think is to learn.

We can never underestimate the true value of knowledge for there has never been an action or thought that hasn't benefited from a source of learning in one way or another. Every right from every wrong; every good from every bad; every gain from every loss; every life from every death - all significant chapters in the story of our eternal existence.

It is vitally important that we appreciate the realities of eternal life before we try to understand the benefits of all knowledge gained from a physical perspective, since it would be extremely naive of us to believe that we can only ever learn from thoughts and actions of a benevolent nature. The moralistic principles instilled within our collective societies dictate that we can only develop both intellectually and spiritually if we practice a healthy and caring lifestyle here on Earth, but sometimes circumstances just don't allow us to function in this salubriously highbrow way.

There is no doubt that life on Earth can seem extremely challenging for anyone born into systematic violence, abuse, extreme hunger or even crippling illness, whilst there is a common view that by simply applying a positive outlook, one can overcome any hardship and find peace and everlasting harmony. Alas, this notion is often flawed in both context and practicality, and the reality is that great joy often only comes after great pain. It is vital that we accept this philosophy before we can start to learn from it.

As we discussed earlier, the legacy that was left behind by Vincent Van Gogh was earned through great personal pain and hardship. His artwork signifies passion and beauty in every sense; however the true wealth of his life on Earth shouldn't be measured in how much money his paintings make at auctions, rather the fact that his work has inspired other artists to create their own masterpieces, no matter the pain and hardship that they personally may find themselves in. True inspiration often comes from those who have paved a path through emotional minefields and discovered greatness from within themselves.

A wise old man once told me about a close friend who committed an act of revulsion in the eyes of many others. This man chose to end the life of his child due to the effects of a debilitating disease. The child was only five years old and had suffered immense physical pain for the entirety of his short life. The father cared for his son as best as he possibly could but he was distraught that he couldn't stop his son's pain despite the child's constant plea for help.

Eventually, the father took away his son's last breath in a desperate attempt to free him from further pain. The repercussions of this act were unsurprisingly devastating for the father and the rest of his family. Society refused to pity the plight of the father and he was convicted of murder and sentenced to life imprisonment.

Many years later, after an attempt to end his own life, the father sat in his prison cell talking to the wise old man. As he wiped away tears riddled with guilt and remorse, the father wondered why his life had been filled with such deep unhappiness. The wise old man looked at the father and smiled. He then placed a hand on the father's shoulder and asked him to close his eyes and think of his son.

As soon as the father closed his eyes, his son appeared in front of him, but now he appeared to be free of pain and happy to see his father. Both the father and son then embraced each other in a loving bond beyond words. The wise old man then suddenly appeared beside both father and son and began to speak decisively. *"The decisions we make are sometimes deemed right or wrong in the eyes of the many, yet decisive in but the eyes of the few. We cannot judge ourselves from what we perceive as acts of kindness or depravity unless we have first experienced the emotional flavour that accompanies such choices, so judge not in others what we cannot judge in truth. In memorandum, there can only ever be one outcome and that is acceptance of what will be... will be."*

As these words echoed away in the distance, the wise old man slowly disappeared with them, leaving the father and son to begin the next part of their eternal journey together.

If we were to examine the life of the father in more detail, what can we deduce from the information given?

The first question we must ask is "Did he have the right to end the life of another human being?" Well, if we were to look at this from both moral and lawful perspectives, then the answer has to be no. But on the other hand, it could be argued that if he hadn't made this choice then both he and his son would have endured a lifetime of physical and emotional pain on Earth. This is clearly a dilemma that is difficult to evaluate when it doesn't directly affect us. There are also so many other factors involved in this case that its complexity will naturally divide opinions. But what we must recognise is that circumstances will change once any soul returns to the spirit dimension. We must also remember that the only judge and jury involved in the spirit dimension is in fact ourselves.

Taking all of this into consideration, it could be considered difficult to chastise the father for his actions, based on the fact that his number one concern was the long term welfare of his son. In reality, we could never truly understand the course of actions taken by the father unless we too were faced with such a life changing predicament.

What is not in doubt though is the fact that the father will have attained a wealth of knowledge from his time spent on Earth, despite the horrendous circumstances surrounding most of it. The question of whether his spiritual passport would be stamped appropriately once returning to the spirit dimension is a matter for both himself and his son. For me or anyone else to judge is utterly pointless.

We have all had moments in this life, or indeed a previous existence, that has made us question ourselves to the point that common sense and decency have become almost redundant. In essence, these are the great challenges in our eternal existence that have shaped the people we have become.

When I first started writing this chapter, I asked my spirit workers to come forward and present me with appropriate and relevant information as I normally would do, but it quickly became apparent that I was hitting my head against a brick wall. I couldn't quite grasp if the link to my guides was somehow temporarily broken or if I was supposed to just write about my own personal experiences and knowledge gained throughout many life journeys. Then, something rather bizarre occurred during a deep meditation that would answer this question...

...There were dozens of small red balls of energy hovering above a large expanse of water. The water was relatively calm with only a slight current travelling in a circular, clockwise motion, yet the scene was dark and mysterious, like a mountain lake glistening softly in the moonlight. The balls of energy lit up the water as they floated like plastic ducks in a bathtub, bobbing from side-to-side as the gentle current sent them in a slow, circular motion. I looked down on them from an elevated position, yet I had no idea where I was nor the purpose of what I was viewing. Until, just in front of me, the image of a man appeared with his back to me, facing the water. I then gazed over his right shoulder as his large hand reached out towards one of the gently circling balls of energy. As his hand reached this particular ball of energy he pushed it gently downwards under the water until it completely disappeared. As he did so, he whispered the word 'healer' and the energy ball was gone from view. The man then reached forward and repeated this act with another ball of energy – pushing it gently downwards under the water and again whispering 'healer' as it also disappeared. At this point, I could not fully understand what I was visualising but deep down I knew that I had to keep watching in expectation of some important message.

As the man reached out for a third time, I intuitively knew which ball of energy he was about to touch this time. Then, as he did so, I felt myself involuntarily floating past him until I was positioned beside the ball of energy. As he pushed this energy ball downwards beneath the lake, I also felt myself being dragged down beside it, as if I was joined to this energy in some way. As I looked up towards the surface of the water, I noticed how it quickly became distant and darker. Then I heard the word 'healer' echoing around me and as I turned around to look at the ball of energy I suddenly realised that it was shaped like a human foetus…

My next recollection was finding myself back sitting in the room of my house – fully conscious and aware of everything around me. I could visibly remember everything that had happened in my meditation, and although the events seemed rather bizarre, I just knew deep within myself that I had just witnessed an indication of my last incarnation to the physical world as a new born baby.

I believe that the relevance of this vision wasn't the fact that my conception took place in this rather peculiar way; it was more the fact that I was given the job of a healer in the forthcoming journey. I also believe that every one of those energy balls left floating on the lake were troubled souls that were in serious need of guidance and enlightenment. For whatever reason, I know that I was one of three souls chosen to return to this Earth to act as envoys for this guide in whatever capacity he chose. In retrospect – three healers returned to Earth to heal others; to heal themselves, and to gain knowledge from all pursuits.

As far as this present physical incarnation is concerned, I do believe that I have been given a specific job to do and I must do it to the best of my abilities. Perhaps this is why my intuitive abilities are superior to most other people, since the need to communicate fluently with my guide is of paramount importance to the success of my spiritual mission.

There is no doubt that people living a physical life have the freedom to make their own choices and decisions which will determine the next step in their eternal existence. But, for me and at least two others, there are some things in life that have to be mapped out for us. Sharing knowledge through the spoken word of the spirit world is undoubtedly one of mine.

My own personal journeys have forever been a mixed bag of truly awful, and thankfully, joyous moments. I know that many periods of my numerous lives in the physical dimension have been tarred by heinous thoughts and actions – yet I have somehow arrived at this precise moment of consciousness that has given me the insight to realise that life is far more complex than simply good versus bad, righteous versus evil, or even rich versus poor. I am also aware that I have endured almost every known emotional experience known to humans – and came out the other side with just the one string to my bow – knowledge!

Knowledge in the spirit dimension could be deemed as wealth, but this wealth is never self-inclusive, it is always shared between everyone who seeks it, and the more who share in this wealth the greater the rewards for everyone involved.

Retrospectively, knowledge in the physical world is usually attributed to masses of information that is stored in the human brain. For example, a University Professor will have amassed a huge amount of knowledge through the natural processes of learning, teaching and discovering – the memories of which are safely stored in a highly-functional brain for the purposes of improving the lives of others. Whereas at the other end of the scale, a new born baby will not have experienced any significant knowledge that is appropriate for functioning in a natural, physical environment. Yet in the spirit world these comparisons will take on a rather different appeal.

When a University Professor returns to the spirit world then all knowledge gained through logical linear mapping will be instantly forgotten since brain matter is not retainable. However, the memories of how this individual was able to achieve great things on Earth through academic attainments will live forever in their spirit consciousness. There is also the small matter of how this individual may have inspired others to achieve their goals, thus creating a repertoire of accomplishments that will personally enhance their chances of attaining accreditation in their spiritual passport.

Nevertheless, it is always life experiences, good or bad, that we take with us into the next step of our conscious awareness. So, let's say for example that our University Professor decides that, despite having learnt everything there is to know about a chosen subject in the life just passed, their personal life suffered deeply as a consequence of this. Should this be the case then they may very well choose another Gap Year back to the physical world in order to try and address this issue, and of course they will naturally begin this next physical existence as a new born baby. Which then begs the question – chicken or egg? The simple answer being that all life is continually progressive. We may find ourselves returning to the physical dimension with a blank canvas of brain power, but inevitably our spiritual consciousness will have automatically benefitted through all physical and emotional life experiences.

The human brain is only a connecting instrument that links the spirit consciousness to the physical body and nerves. The brain is simply the engine of our car. The hands and feet of the body instruct the engine on how fast or slow to power the wheels. But it is our imaginative spirit consciousness that shapes every journey that we take – and the memories of where these journeys take us lie forever in our eternal life path.

Life does indeed create many up's and down's in our eternal quest to find answers to endless questions. Perhaps we should all view life from the perspective of a new born baby; slowly descending from the dark, chilling waters of our innermost thoughts, in preparation for the journey of a lifetime.

CHAPTER 6

Every soul has the ability to share love

Love – a four letter word that is widely thought to heal every known discomfort that you could ever possibly imagine. But what is the true definition of love in terms of spiritual values? More importantly, how will we know when we have truly found spiritual love?

Only when the answer to every prayer is forgiven.

Only when the weight of enforced solitude is shared.

Only when the darkness that clouds compassion is pardoned.

Only when the manacles of suppression are fully released.

Only when winds that howl bring breath through stifled hearts.

Only when the reason for disapproval fulfils many causes.

Only when the voices of a fellowship sing louder than the choirs that preach fame, fortune and glorified salvation.

And only when the smallest, most gentlest of souls carries your burden through perils of self-enforced disharmony, no matter where, when, why or how.

Only then... can you ever contemplate the unequivocal beauty of true unbridled love.

The great Scottish poet, Alexander Smith, stated that '*Love is but the discovery of ourselves in others, and the delight in the recognition.*' I would recommend that you read this quote several times and just let those words sink into your spirit consciousness for a few moments. Don't try and analyse those words, rather let them bed themselves neatly in your mind so that they may remind you of everything that has ever truly mattered to you throughout a lifetime of perceived failures and accomplishments. In essence – that is the real power of love, and however hard you may try to fight it, you can never escape from it.

There is a common perception shared by many people that certain individuals who have committed crimes of hate upon other human beings are devoid of experiencing love. This is simply not possible. Even individuals who have committed mass murder will have experienced love from others at some point in their lives. Likewise, they will almost certainly have loved someone as well, despite their turbulent existence. Nobody has ever been born a mass murderer – this is a tenure earned through continuous misguided thoughts and physical feelings.

It is still possible to have your spiritual passport stamped and authorised after committing heinous crimes against society – if it wasn't then there would be no point in coming here in the first place. However, it is imperative that any soul fully accepts the consequences of their actions before recommencing their spiritual journey. This feat can only be achieved by searching for love in others and in ourselves.

Love, as poetically described by Alexander Smith, is always there for us; remaining close by, even though we may often feel that it has deserted us. For every soul that has strayed from their chosen path, another soul is always ready to reach out and carry them back to the straight and narrow, no matter the circumstances that led to that soul becoming astray.

Of course, the task of achieving righteousness is always made easier in the spirit dimension, as the reality of past demeanours finally becomes much more obvious. Nevertheless, the task is never easy and can create immense feelings of shame and remorse that require softening and gentle nurturing. The best way to achieve this is to grasp love and begin to cherish it. Then, once healing has commenced, a new journey will open up new opportunities and tortured souls will eventually be rejuvenated through the power of unconditional love.

There is a rather funny looking little rodent currently gracing the grasslands of America, that has a peculiar pastime that often baffles, yet then again, amazes anyone who is fortunate enough to witness it. I am, of course, referring to the Prairie Dog – a squirrel-like creature with many human-like characteristics and behaviours. Noted for their ecological virtues – they build underground colonies that create shelter for many other neighbouring creatures; Prairie Dogs are often regarded as the "Chicken McNuggets" of the local populous due to being a key food source for many larger predators. So, in a sense, they are a key element of the evolutionary cycle of many creatures in this part of the world.

So what makes these chubby-looking mammals so interesting compared to other species in our vast habitat? Well, they live in close-knit family gatherings – their dwelling places are aptly called Prairie Dog Towns – and animal research has found that Prairie Dogs communicate with intricate detail in a way that human beings normally would as opposed to other species of the animal kingdom. They will constantly make alternating sounds to alert others of impending danger, depending on whoever or whatever is threatening them. In fact, many scientists believe that these animals have their very own unique language and can communicate so effectively with each other that eventually even humans may begin to fully understand them.

To put this into perspective, if no one really knows what language is or how it originated in humans, then the existence of language within these creatures is even more baffling, yet incredibly fascinating. Perhaps, there is more to learn from them than there is from any of us.

But that's not all. An additional element to Prairie Dog behaviour that we often find perplexing is their ability to kiss each other like humans do. Animal behaviourists have studied these animals with particular fascination as they lock teeth to greet each other in a way that no other creature does. It is presumed that this form of greeting is to ascertain whether certain individuals are part of their intricate family group – perhaps a long, lost cousin returning from a Gap Year no less. But it is worth taking into cognizance that if the language and communication skills of Prairie Dogs are so good, then it could be argued that they wouldn't really need to kiss each other in order to know exactly who was who.

There is another facet of this behaviour that many people consider to be true. Could it just be that they are simply showing a sign of affection when greeting each other? Perhaps just like a simple kiss between human beings to show that there is a common bond or courteous appreciation between them? We will never truly know unless the language barrier between us is successfully broken down, yet for all the study that's been made in regards to the animals that grace our world, wouldn't it be rather obtuse of us to believe that they are incapable of showing emotions; or displaying affection, or even loving one another the way we do.

It's not just Prairie Dogs that have an ability to express themselves in such a manner as to exude emotion. In fact, every creature on Earth has this inherent ability. And why wouldn't they? What would be the point in generating a life here on Earth if it meant simply wandering about looking for food before being gobbled up by a bigger animal with the exact same philosophy?

That would be a rather crass viewpoint that hinted on the superiority of human existence, where all other species only existed for our own amusement or curiosity.

Since becoming more aware of my own ability to communicate with spirit energies, I have also discovered an ability to connect with dogs. I have found that dogs can converse telepathically with each other and that occasionally I also have the ability to link into this.

One example of this occurred when a friend of mine returned from their local Veterinary Surgery with the tragic news that her beloved pet dog would need to be put to sleep as a large mass on the animal's stomach could not be explained. Not only was the dog not feeling particularly well; it was elderly and had been refusing food, so naturally the Vet presumed that it had lost the will to live due to the affliction. As I spoke to my friend, I started to visualise the dog sending images to me of a human being with a similar mass on their stomach. I could then see the word Diverticulitis in my mind. Then, before I knew it, I was instructing my friend to go back to the surgery and demand an x-ray of the dog's stomach. Incredibly, the dog immediately began to perk up and wag his tail, almost as if he was breathing a sigh of relief.

My friend informed me some time later that the dog did indeed have Diverticulitis – a human disorder that can very rarely affect dogs. Thankfully, he made a full recovery.

On reflection, I just presumed that my spiritual guides had informed me of the dog's illness. Yet, I couldn't understand why the dog suddenly perked up whenever I mentioned the diagnosis. It was as if he knew himself what was wrong with him and that it wasn't as serious as first presumed.

Maybe it's not just Dr Doolittle that talks to the animals. Perhaps we all have this inner ability to share thoughts and feelings with every creature on Earth. After all, most of us talk to our pets as if we expect them to know what we are saying. My own pet dog Oscar, a fox red Labrador with a penchant for food, walks and... more food, often waits for me to say the "magic words" before scurrying off to look for his food bowl or his walking harness. However, sometimes I only need to look at him and visualise his food bowl or his harness - and he knows, he just knows. They all do, it's only our high moral compass that prevents most of us from believing it to be true.

We can therefore assume that if dogs can display emotions, feelings and the coherent ability to communicate with each other then surely they have the faculty to express true feelings of love, even on an equal with us humans. And if all living creatures possess this desire to share feelings with each other then it is conceivable to assume that they can also share these feelings with us humans.

Perhaps, when Prairie Dogs kiss in the presence of us humans, it is performed to show us that we are not the only species who have the ability to express deep emotion. Or, in the poetic words of Alexander Smith, they are just delighting in the recognition of themselves in others, or the recognition of themselves in us.

As human beings we have a duty to protect all species from harm. We do not have to fall in love with our animals – just respect them, and we may just truly discover ourselves.

CHAPTER 7

I am the creator of all that is truthful

Truth is a word that regularly invokes a vast debate in regards to both moral and subjective opinions. To tell the truth can often signify an admission of guilt in those individuals who may have committed an act of self-treachery. Likewise, a small white lie can sometimes be deemed ethically appropriate when attempting to conceal an awful fact that may subjectively affect someone in a state of personal turmoil.

Nevertheless, truthfulness in the eyes of our spiritual teachers and elders is a concept that should always be given the utmost importance throughout our perennial wellbeing. In modern times, it has become extremely easy to tell a lie to someone and not feel an ounce of guilt as society has now found itself governed by individuals and organisations that have become adept at withholding truthful or factual information. Furthermore, our cultures have now become a quintessential playground for ordinary people wishing to express feelings of being bullied or overlooked in favour of others who may fit in better with more populous beliefs or social standings. In turn, this has created a blame culture that has spawned an odious need for legal representation with a commercial bounty in tow for the seemingly loudest complainer. In short, it is often more beneficial to hold back information if it means not being sued or being accused of any kind of back-door nepotism.

In retrospect, we shouldn't really generalise this current state of affairs, since we have already alluded to the fact that we will only ever be judged on our own actions when the time comes for spiritual evaluation. With this in mind, perhaps we should concentrate more specifically on the reasons as to why we may choose to lie to someone, and decide on whether the intention is to deceive them or to simply shelter them from physical or emotional harm.

Lying is an art that is indigenous to human beings. Our use of spoken or visual language as a means of communication opens up a plethora of different forms of manipulation that can easily deceive our minds. For example, we often purchase consumer goods after viewing, hearing or reading an advertisement that makes an item sound far more appealing than it actually is, or even convincing us that we really need this product when in actual fact it brings little benefit to our well-being. The reality is that the advertiser has used ingenious techniques to convey a message to our susceptible minds that makes us desire the need to improve our lives, and buying this product stimulates a need to adhere to this extremely compelling system.

This form of selling may not fall directly into the category of dishonesty, since it is closely monitored by Consumer Protection laws. However, if the intent of such a practice is to conceal any weaknesses or flaws within the product then you start to walk a fine line between the hidden scruples of integrity and deceit.

Here's a fact - spirit mediums who work with higher energies in the spiritual domain make lousy salespeople, since we have an inability to deceive consumers that makes selling luxury items extremely difficult. We will often go to painstaking methods to point out everything and anything that may or may not benefit the consumer, and although this may sound like an honest and fair customer-friendly supposition, the reality is that the customer usually doesn't want to buy something that won't give them the stimulation they desperately crave. Furthermore, if we did momentarily fall off the wagon and sell a huge Hummer truck to a little old lady with a Zimmer frame, then I can guarantee you that our consciences would suffer greatly afterwards until we could make it right.

Spirit mediums are not perfect human beings; we don't have an inbuilt integrity meter that prevent us from lying or deceiving people, nor do we possess a self-righteous persona that automatically makes us look down on anyone else struggling to make a living through whatever means possible. It's simply a fact that we have a stronger awareness and connection to those energies who cannot detract from the absolute truth in any form of communication between us, and their heavy influence in our decision making bears greatly on our systemic existence here on Earth. The reason for this is actually quite logical.

In the spirit world, where there is no physical mass in existence, the only means of communication is through telepathy. In other words, to communicate with another life form, you must openly express your thoughts and they will be automatically received and interpreted in the exact same format that they were presented. For example, if you were to ask for help from someone then they would automatically understand what you needed help for – and it wouldn't be to sell them a brand new Hummer! In other words, there is no way that communication in this form can be misinterpreted, and if you were to attempt to lie to someone then they would instantly realise this due to being able to read your thoughts.

In summary, it is impossible to lie to someone through telepathic communication, so when we return to the spiritual dimension then we can either practice what we have previously been preaching in the physical world, or drastically readjust to this seamless way of social interaction. It is for this reason that spiritual guides will always advocate truthfulness above all other virtues. It is imperative that we at least consider the environment that we will all eventually discover (or in most cases rediscover) and appreciate that truth between souls is even more important than love.

I stated before that lying is indigenous to the human race and this proclamation is based on the fact that animals also communicate telepathically. Prairie Dogs already know the thoughts of those who are about to be kissed. Domestic dogs may often be misled by their owners but that is only because they are used to hearing particular sounds which usually mean a specific thing. They cannot be deceived by other animals – that is impossible. It is, as previously stated, only humans who can display this trait.

When we return to the spiritual dimension with our passport in hand, we will resume our education in a classroom where only truth and rectitude will suffice. Our resultant review of the physical life just passed will open up the challenge of justifying each action, regardless of whether you were totally honest in your actions. It is the karmic law of "cause and intent" that adjudicates each task and this will give you the tools to make judgement on yourself. If you have caused great strife to another individual through deceit, then you will now have the opportunity to be honest about the reasons why you chose to do this. Whereas, deceit may have caused the problem, honesty can now resolve it. Anything else will always have grave consequences.

Oscar Wilde once said "The truth is rarely pure and never simple." Perhaps he based this statement on the fact that the truth is often far more frightening than a simple lie, bearing in mind that fears are such an integral part of today's society. Perhaps we need to find a way of removing these fears and allowing truth to become a simpler and more rewarding part of physical life that encourages us to be open and honest without fear of offending each other.

A wise old man once told me to close my eyes and imagine a world that promised so much yet delivered so little.

He said that on a clear day I could see for miles, but when the sun refused to shine then I could see even further.

He said that when the ghosts appeared to me, I hid in the shadows for protection; yet when the unseen touched my hand, I shook with excitement.

He said that when the people cried for help, I held out a healing hand, even though I yearned for salvation when self-madness struck.

He said that the love lost as a child could only return when I acknowledged that love is ageless, timeless and everlasting.

He said that if I closed my eyes then my world would always appear as I desired it to be; either with fear, dread and disdain; or with purpose, courtesy and intent.

He said that when I opened my eyes then all I would be left with was the truth – that what was being created in my mind was everything that I ever needed to truly find myself.

A wise old man once told me to create a world that promised so much yet delivered so little – and all I created was truthful.

Truth, in itself, is a word that is used in many contexts in our day to day physical existence. Its purpose and intent is measured in our legal practices and in many of our religious beliefs. We are taught from an early age that if you don't tell the truth to our peers then we will never gain respect and admiration as adults. We are also constantly reminded that law and order is dependent on a truthful society that cannot function progressively in any other format. However, despite all of these ethical instructions our society is still riddled with deceit and in general is becoming more and more untrustworthy in many facets of everyday living.

As individuals it is not our mission to change society's way of thinking. It is not our job to preach the ways of our spiritual fathers to renounce dishonesty in any shape or fashion. Nor is it our task to judge others for not heeding to a strict code of morals.

We will only ever be judged by ourselves when we return to the higher dimensions. We can only ever create our own world around us – and it is within our own world that we will all create our own truths.

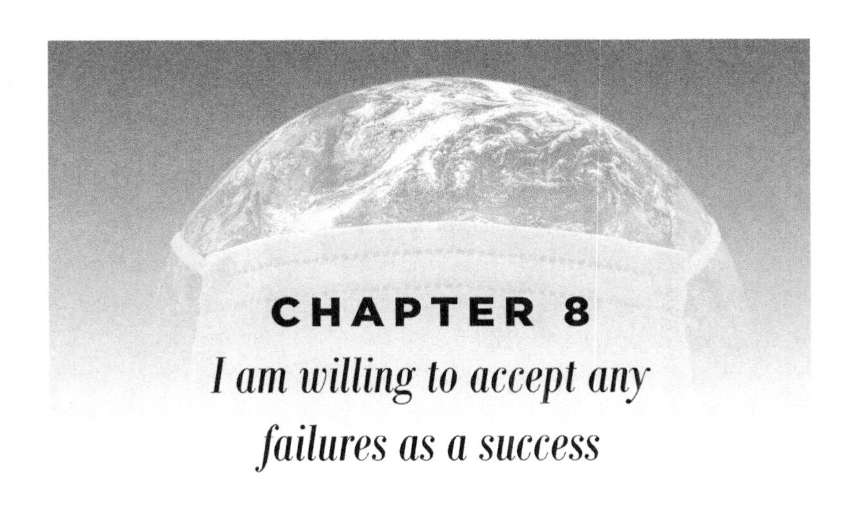

CHAPTER 8

I am willing to accept any failures as a success

"The secret of success is having tripped over every hurdle and enjoyed the experience of getting back up and tripping over even more"

David Shaw 2015.

It's now 11:40 am on the 1st April 2020 and almost five years have passed since I wrote the first few words of this "new" book. In that time I have lived a life that hasn't exactly set the world on fire in terms of achieving any academic or socially-inspired achievements. Having said that, there have been some significant ups and downs that have made me question myself as a human being and also as a servant of my spiritual elders. Furthermore, there has recently been a significant change to the world's energy force that has made me stand up and take a good look at myself and question whether I should be more active in helping others in times of great hardship.

The problem is that I genuinely do want to help people as much as I can, but there comes a time when everyone has to realise that life is but a great test and it is a much better thing that we do to face this test ourselves than allow others do this for us.

According to my spiritual elders, it is written in the great universal scriptures that life is wholly based on personal challenges, not just from a small perspective but also of a much larger scale. Yet, despite these challenges being viewed as either small or large, they should always be treated with equal importance, regardless of the potential consequences to one's self or mankind as a whole. However, we must also understand that to test oneself in the eyes of another is fruitless as only the challenges of a self-ordained soul will effectively carry merit in an eternal existence.

Much has been written about success in the physical world through fields such as sport, acting, singing, dancing, business and many other diverse competitive activities ranging from "Rear of the Year" to "Best Haircut in a Soap Opera". It really is a morally challenging world if you look at it from this rather perverse angle, with the constant need for self-assurance in a covetous social platform ensuring that this market remains vibrant in context, if not ethics.

I will now present several examples of sporting feats where personal success has been appreciated so much more because of countless failures from the past. The first case is tennis player Andy Murray. Andy was hoping to become the first male British tennis player to win a major grand slam title for over 70 years, but despite becoming one of the world's top players he just couldn't seem to accomplish this ambition. Four times he reached the final of these prestigious events and four times he lost, before finally winning the US Open in 2012. The scenes at the end of his victory were truly magical as every spectator watching, at both the event and on television, shared a highly emotional moment. Andy had previously been widely criticised after losing his previous finals, with the media and sporting industry critics questioning whether he really had a winner's mentality or had settled for being branded as just a glorious runner-up. The pressure became so great that Andy broke down in tears after losing his first Wimbledon final in 2012, only weeks before his triumphant win in America.

Andy would then go on to win Wimbledon twice in the next four years – a feat he dreamed of when growing up as a young tennis hopeful in Scotland, but it's his inaugural win in 2012 that he will be best remembered for. Sometimes it takes many great failures to truly appreciate any kind of success. Without those failures, his win in 2012 would surely not have meant so much to him.

The second sporting example is that of golfer Tiger Woods. Tiger dominated this sport from 1997 onwards, winning fourteen major titles and becoming by far the best golfer in that time period. In fact, many golfing enthusiasts got so fed up with Tiger winning everything that his popularity began to wane dramatically. After winning his 14th title in 2008, his personal life became a huge struggle, coupled by a procession of serious back injuries. His career looked to be over as his game suffered and he was no longer the great threat to other top players that he once was.

In 2019, whilst competing in the US Masters at Augusta, his game suddenly started to click together. With only one round to go, Tiger was nicely placed just behind the leader. Incredibly, he ended up winning the tournament by just the one shot and the scenes at the end were reminiscent of the aftermath of Andy Murray's first triumph. Tiger had already won more golf tournaments than any other player in the game's history, bar one, but this victory was special in its own unique way because Tiger had been written off by everyone – in golf and also in life in general. In retrospect, it was only himself that believed he could once again win a major tournament after eleven years of personal turmoil and mediocre golf.

Tiger's life, by his own admission, had been like an out of control rollercoaster for so many years and many of the game's most loyal advocates had already turned their back on this once great sportsman. Now they stood and applauded with tears welling in their eyes as Tiger humbly hugged his family after winning the Masters. He would later say that this victory was by far his greatest ever triumph and he dedicated it to his family, who had faithfully stood by him and inspired him.

Perhaps Tiger had felt that his great record at golf tournaments had being overshadowed or consumed by his personal crisis. Who knows what made his game suddenly so good at this tournament? The only thing we can safely say is that his success at this event was made so much sweeter by what had gone on beforehand.

Sometimes we can often feel that we have achieved everything in life by being better than everyone else, only to find that we have accomplished very little; but we have already alluded to the fact that life is about experiences, good or bad, successful or not. Finding the perfect balance between the two will offer us the best opportunity to assess ourselves and appreciate the journey of others.

Any failures in life should always be regarded as merely a part of any triumphs. After all, there is no yin without yang; no cause without effect; no rich without poor; no sun without rain; no love without hate; no night without day, and no light can ever exist without darkness. Savour both and I promise that you will experience fulfilment in abundance.

Now that we have considered the merits of failures and achievements in the physical world, let us concentrate on the more important aspects of eternal life. As previously discussed, we have all arrived back on this physical plane with certain goals in mind, and it is these objectives that must be assessed when we return to self-judgement in the spirit dimension. We know that money, power or social status has no bearing in a world where equality reigns supreme, so we can therefore presume that winning golf or tennis tournaments can only ever be regarded as an experience. It's how you later deal with this experience that determines whether it could be classed as a personal success.

At the 2016 World Triathlon Championship in Mexico, Jonny Brownlee from Great Britain was leading the final stage run with only 400 meters to go when he started to falter badly and could barely even stand up. His brother Alistair was lying in second place and when he caught up with Jonny he chose to help his brother struggle over the finish line instead of just running past him to claim victory and be crowned World Champion.

Meanwhile, another athlete had run past both brothers to claim victory, with the Brownlee's crossing the line shortly afterwards in second and third place respectively. If you are a fan of Triathlon then you may know the name of the victor. Everyone else just remembers the brothers crossing the line in glorious failure. It was an iconic moment in the history of the sport that will be long remembered.

Success is often measured in not what you can do for yourself, but what you can do for others. Likewise, failure is often measured by what you failed to do for others, rather than what you failed to achieve for yourself.

"We are all failures – at least the best of us are."

J.M Barrie.

CHAPTER 9

I am no more impressive than the humblest hobo

The American civil rights activist, Jesse Jackson, once proclaimed that we should never look down on anyone unless we are helping them up. As much as this powerful message helps us to realise that equality is fundamental in ensuring the existence of a fair-minded society, I've always preferred the concept of kneeling down beside a person before offering to help them up. Looking down on someone before helping them up could imply that you were simply doing them a favour and this could perhaps represent an action that would make you feel more important or more powerful than the person who accepts your help. It really depends on your own interpretation of such an event, but as we know, our world has suddenly become a haven for discerning individuals with too many plastic axes to grind.

The media world has become heavily populated with people attempting to create a public persona that reflects an ignominious feeling of self-importance. This narcissistic culture requires a constant focus on an individual's every action or opinion, and often their profile will need suitably boosted if criticism arises from those who are much less captivated by this perverse form of social manipulation. The inane solution is to show this individual in a more embellishing light – for example as a caring, sincere individual who wishes to share his or her successful lifestyle with their adoring fans. This can be achieved by a number of means and there are ready-made teams of professional media consultants and public relations specialists who are adept at fashioning iconic characters who often bear little resemblance to the fans who worship them.

You often have to wonder why those doting fans would want to admire someone who has drifted so far away from reality that any connection between them would seem distant and surreal – almost God-like. Moreover, if this media megastar was to look down on you before holding out a hand to help you up, then you may question whether their honourable intention was to truly help you, or rather benefit their own public image.

The best-selling book of all time is The Bible. Written thousands of years ago, when the world's inhabitants were easily influenced by numerous forms of subservient worship, our hero – Jesus, enjoyed a brief but memorable status as a leading light of humanity. Looked upon by many as a saviour of mankind, Jesus addressed the need for salvation to all humans in a time of great human hardship. However, unlike many other preachers of that time or indeed since his existence, it was written that he refused to be worshipped as anything other than an ordinary man. Perhaps this is why this book has remained so popular throughout our recent history. The overall message it portrays is that Jesus himself regarded himself as no more important than the humblest of hobos. Nevertheless, the vast majority of people who follow the words of The Bible and dedicate their lives to the memory of Jesus Christ still regard him as some sort of superstar or miracle worker who has the ability to save us all from ourselves with just one click of his fingers.

Have you ever wondered what Jesus would think of his new found popularity if he was to return to Earth today, and more importantly whether today's world was in his eyes a better place to live than the one he left behind two thousand years ago? Maybe he would find that not much has changed.

A wise old man once told me that he had developed the power to see into his own future. He informed me that this new found ability was helping him to decide where and when to invest his money so that he could live a life of luxury akin to other souls with a similar disposition to himself. He added that if I was to join with him in this prosperous crusade then I too would benefit from having a prior knowledge of upcoming events and could make decisions which allowed me to feel better about myself.

However, the wise old man then advised me that there would be one thing that I needed to do before I could join him in this quest. He said that I had to leave behind everything that was holding me back, including any friends or family that were constantly relying on me for their own welfare.

I thought about this for a while, contemplating whether I really needed friends and family who were so selfish, knowing that I would meet new acquaintances once my lifestyle had been upgraded to a more salubrious calibre.

The wise old man then placed his hands on my shoulders and offered me a preview of this new found glorious existence. As I took a deep breath, I felt a sense of self-satisfaction running through me that I hadn't ever felt before. This strange sensation engulfed me as I visualised a world where everyone looked up to me with adulation. I felt like a prince who had slain the pauper with a lance made of solid gold. I was being lauded by the mightiest of swordsmen and the loveliest of noblewomen, all proclaiming my arrival as an event that enhanced their own self-worth.

As I then began to gaze around this palace of enchantment, I suddenly noticed that the wise old man who had accompanied me on this glorious journey was now much younger and more handsome than before. He seemed to be enjoying this sense of fulfilment every bit as much as I was.

He then looked at me for what seemed like an eternity, before I suddenly noticed the smile slowly disappearing from his face. His body then began to wither as if it was being dragged down through the earth below his feet. He reached out a hand and asked for my help. I looked around for guidance and all of my new found friends instructed me to let him go as he wasn't worth it, and he would only drag me back down to where I had originally came from. I stopped for a moment, my thoughts swirling in a tumultuous wind of confusion, searching for righteousness in a sea of contempt.

As the wise old man drifted down into the earth, I knelt down and offered him my hand just before he completely disappeared. Our hands met just in time, before he left this place, and I then found myself back where I had originally started. My friends and family were already waiting for me. They had witnessed the demise of the wise old man and they were ready to support my grief, unlike the inhabitants of the other, more ostentatious place that I had witnessed through Adam's snake-shadowed eyes.

I now realised that I had made the correct decision. Here was my place of comfort in times of need. Here was my destiny, despite visions of grandeur enticing me to a place where only strangers would meet. Here was my future, where wise old men stayed old and wise, and where broken hearts stayed broken but loved.

To be able to return to the spirit dimension as nothing more than the humblest of hobos is but a great feat of mankind. To do so as a result of having refuted all forms of social self-importance is a remarkable achievement regardless of whether any other goals have not yet been met. Any soul returning to the spirit dimension with nothing more than a conscience to declare at the customs desk, will find that they will have fewer questions to answer when the time for self-evaluation occurs.

We all wish for the best for ourselves and our families in a world that rarely rewards anyone who stands at the back of the queue. It can be a difficult place in which to thrive when seemingly only the loudest, brashest people appear to achieve the most in a highly covetous fashion. Regardless of this, every living being in any dimension, physical or spiritual, is important in its own right. If it wasn't important then it would cease to exist.

Remember, it's what's important to you that matters, not what others deem to be important about you; then, when those who are important to you reach out a hand for assistance, never look down upon them. Instead, consider kneeling down to their appropriate level, where they feel as comfortable as you do, before offering support in a way that they will understand and trust on an even keel.

The humblest of minds are the ones that neither seek nor find any greater worth than what you eventually leave with.

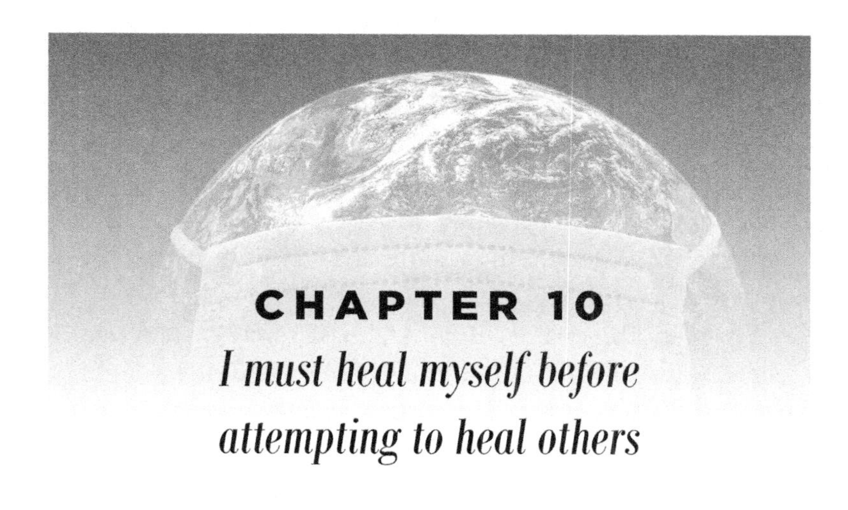

CHAPTER 10
I must heal myself before attempting to heal others

When most of us think of the art of healing, our minds are automatically then drawn towards images of hospitals, doctors, nurses, pharmaceutical drugs or several days propped up in bed with just a hot water bottle as our sole companion. In many ways, those instruments of recovery are usually enough to return us back to a common symptom-free sense of normality, but in the not so distant past, the human body relied on a very different, more natural form of healing power. That power being the humble touch of human hands.

I have to confess that I've never really been a fully committed exponent of spiritual healing to the extent that I have been able to heal physical ailments that have afflicted either me personally or that of others. This has often surprised me due to the fact that I have been working with higher energies through trance mediumship, yet whenever I have questioned this with trance guides, I have always been furnished with the same response – we all work in different ways using different strengths and the art of healing has many different meanings within the physical world.

With this analogy in mind, I have rarely ever offered healing to anyone unless they have specifically sought out my help. Not that I would ever refuse anybody, but I usually prefer to recommend the services of other spiritual workers that specialise in the healing of the physical body.

As a psychotherapist, I meet many people who suffer from stress and depression and this is where my spiritual workers can help. Having personally gone through both of these debilitating conditions, I always feel that I can relate to people who have lost control of their state of mind. I suppose it's a bit like what we discussed in the last chapter – kneeling down to help someone up. My spirit workers also continually remind me that a person needs to be of sound mind before they can heal their body, so in a way this form of healing could sometimes be even more important than healing physical ailments.

Throughout my many physical years of spiritual education I have participated in various forms of healing courses and development studies, most of which have come beautifully packaged and presented, and made me feel spiritually and emotionally enlightened. All of them have shown me various conceptions of the human body and soul and made me question my own techniques and understanding of the human touch. However, they all profess one single common attribute – you must heal yourself of all physical and mental distractions before attempting to work on other people.

The biggest mistake that we spiritual healers make is to forget to work on ourselves regularly – and I will admit that I am one of the worst culprits. Spiritual healers often believe that their sole mission in life is to help as many people as possible and this is an undertaking that often leads to complete physical and mental exhaustion. We are, after all, only human beings and the stresses of everyday living will affect us as much as we choose to let them. Our guides can only ever do so much to keep us from hardship but there comes a time when we have to rest and regenerate our energy appropriately.

In essence, we must regularly heal ourselves before attempting to heal others. As previously stated, I began writing this book over five years ago. Unfortunately, I had to cease writing as I suffered from what many authors call "writers block". The reality was that I was struggling to connect with my spiritual writers and unbeknown to me I would need to take some time off before recommencing my journey. It would take me a further five years before I felt that I could connect in a way that truly meant something to me and to anyone who reads these words. I now feel fully prepared for the next step in my eternal life journey. This is the story of the last five years.

Whenever I used to pick up my parents for a leisurely drive to the local supermarket or coffee house, I would often drive them home via somewhere that they used to live near or frequent when they were much younger. We would comment on how the landscape or surroundings had changed throughout the years and reminisce about the "good old days" when life seemed so much simpler and less demanding.

My dad would smile but say very little – he was always a man who preferred to look forward rather than look back, although he would always admit that he enjoyed life much more when he was a younger man. My mum, on the other hand, would love to talk about her childhood days when everyone pulled together and embraced whatever life threw at them, no matter the circumstances. Life for her was always so much more appealing when her parents and their extended family were still alive.

I suppose it was a gradual thing when both my dad and I began to notice that my mum would only ever recollect memories from her distant past, and not memories from her recent past. We didn't think too much of it as she seemed happy to relive those cherished moments from her childhood, even though we would hear those same stories over and over again. Then, all of a sudden, my mum started to have really bad days when she couldn't complete anything that she had started doing around her house, yet on other days she was perfectly lucid and totally unaware that her short-term memory was beginning to deteriorate.

After a short spell in hospital my mum's memory was tested by consultant psychiatrists to determine whether she had the capacity to make comprehensible decisions to support her welfare. The result was devastating for my family. Hospital staff recommended that my mum was placed in a care home as soon as possible for her own and my dad's best interests. It was a rapid decline in my mum's health and I was stunned at how quickly she had deteriorated to the extent that she could no longer stay in her own home.

Dementia is a condition that doesn't have specific tests to determine whether you are ill or not. It's a cognitive state of mind that has to be evaluated by experts in this field, who then make a judgement call. This can be very difficult for families to accept as there are days when your loved one seems perfectly normal and yet you are being told that something horrible is eating away at them and there is no hope of recovery.

As a psychotherapist, I have often had clients come to me after having been diagnosed with schizophrenia. They have previously been told by psychiatrists that this is a lifelong condition requiring constant medication that will try to keep them functioning as best as possible in a normal world. When they then come to me I immediately inform them that they are not mentally ill – rather they are normal people living in a crazy world, and they are just questioning whether this crazy world needs to be as crazy as it is. Together, we work with our minds and discover that the truth is often more frightening than the make believe. Most of these clients then eventually return to what society deems as a normal way of living after their psychiatrist reduces their medication appropriately.

To the same extent, whenever I am asked if someone with dementia knows what their loved one is trying to say to them, I always state that they know exactly what's going on – it's only our lack of awareness that prevents us from realising this. My own ability to communicate telepathically with sufferers of this condition has reinforced my viewpoint.

Therefore, as someone who has a great respect for experts in psychiatry, but who hasn't necessarily always agreed with certain viewpoints and treatments, I was initially somewhat sceptical of the diagnosis given to my mum. However, I could not come up with any other solution as I suddenly realised that in this instance, I now wasn't a therapist treating a client. On the one hand, I was a son trying to help his family, but in my view failing miserably. On the other hand, my family weren't looking for a therapist who could talk about the ins and outs of everyday living – they were looking for someone to fix the problem, and I couldn't. Therefore, we were all at the mercy of people we needed to trust implicitly to look after us and we had to abide by their expertise and decision making.

Subsequently, my mum spent several months in a nursing home and she hated it. My dad, my uncle and I would take her out regularly to various places of interest but inevitably when we returned to the nursing home my mum would be inconsolable. It reminded me of the time when my wife and I first took our son to the nursery school and he would be screaming at us not to leave him there. The nursery teachers would comment that he would be fine in a few moments. The care home staff said the same about my mum. Deep down though, I knew that they both would never get used to being left alone.

When my mum was admitted to hospital after falling into a diabetic coma, my dad and I were informed that she would not recover. The doctor suspected sepsis and advised that she shouldn't be given any treatment. After three days had passed my mum opened her eyes and looked at me. She couldn't talk but I knew what she was trying to say. She was ready to go home and relive her childhood memories with her parents.

After five days of waiting on my mum to pass over, I awoke one morning in my house with my spirit guides all around me. I was informed that it was now time for my mum's passing. I telephoned my sister and let her know of the situation. She would leave right away and be with us in around ninety minutes from her home in the Scottish Borders. I arrived at the hospital and the staff confirmed that my mum was at the last stage of her life. She passed to spirit just a few minutes after my sister arrived.

Our immediate feelings were of relief. Our mum had suffered terribly for the last few months and now she could relax without pain or fear. I knew that she would be well looked after in spirit but I still retained mixed emotions of guilt and shame. I felt guilty that I hadn't questioned care home staff more on whether she was being adequately looked after. Likewise, I also questioned myself on whether I could have done more before she ended up in permanent care. In hindsight, my only real concern was that after all that had happened, did my mum know that I truly loved her. I hope she now knows that I do. I just wish that I had more opportunities to tell her that.

My dad passed away just over a year later. He too began to suffer from memory relapses. In truth, he never really recovered from losing my mum. He spent his last few months living near to my sister in a lovely sheltered housing complex. He had everything to live for, but nobody special to share it with.

He was also given only a few days to live after being admitted to hospital and then diagnosed with terminal cancer. I awoke one morning and was informed by my guides that my dad was leaving this world very shortly. My sister phoned to say that the hospital had also phoned her with the same opinion. As I drove the twenty miles to the hospital I was told by my guides to slow down as they were holding back my father's passing until both my sister and I arrived to be at his bedside.

We both arrived to find my dad not breathing. My sister asked me if he was dead but I asked her to wait for confirmation. My dad then suddenly took two more breaths before passing over to spirit to be beside my mum. It was a traumatic time for my family so soon after my mum's death. In all honesty, we had hardly got over my mum's death before my dad started to fall ill. We tried to give him all the love and attention that we could but he just missed my mum so much and in the end died of a broken heart.

My parents had both died within two years of each other. I always wondered what grief would consist of after the death of a loved one. I'm still not entirely sure. I do know that both of them visit me regularly and try to advise me on certain matters, so I can only presume that in some respects you never really stop being a parent.

It has taken me some time to be able to come to terms with their passing. Sometimes you just need to find yourself before any healing can begin. I hope that any reader who can relate to what I have just written can begin their own healing process.

Healing yourself can be the one of the greatest challenges that any soul undertakes. That is the main reason that we choose to return to the physical world. We can only ever evolve once the pain of our past in any dimension or timeline is addressed, understood and relieved with pure love. I now hope these words will help to heal my own eternal life.

CHAPTER 11

I am but one small part of the evolution of eternal life

As a child growing up in a small town in the northwest of the United Kingdom, I enjoyed a simple life based on playing sports with my friends, watching old Elvis movies with my mum, and arguing with my dad about whether his musical tastes from the 60's were better or worse than mine from the 80's.

Daytime activities were always active and frivolous to the extent that whenever bedtime came around I would easily fall into a profound, wholesome sleep pattern – at least for a few hours or so. More often than not though, I would briefly find myself in a peculiar world of mystery and horror as I drifted between sporadic periods of deep sleep and lucid dreaming.

The nightmares started when I was about seven years old. A seemingly innocuous dream state would be abruptly interrupted by a mysterious stranger who would stalk me in my journey from one random place to another. He would continually remain just out of sight but I knew that he was close by, waiting to pounce on me – and he usually did. Strangely though, I would immediately find myself being transported back to the safe haven of my bedroom as soon as he got close to me, convincing me that I had in fact woken up from the nightmare and was no longer being threatened. Alas, I would suddenly hear him walking slowly up my hall staircase before entering my room and I would finally see him clearly, as he menacingly stood over me with a large dagger in his hand. Fear would instinctively make me close my eyes tight, hoping that he would just leave me alone.

Mercifully, I found that if I could somehow just relax for a few seconds and focus my attention on something other than my impending fate, that I could brusquely shout out at the intruder and he would thankfully disappear. In hindsight, I never ever felt his knife touch my body but the fear of this attack was always enough to terrify me during each and every episode. Sometimes I would shout out at him as normal and find myself back in my bed, shaken but relieved that he was gone. Then, for some reason I would discover that I was still stuck in a deep state of trance and my attacker would return with his knife in hand, determined to finish me off. After shouting out again and finding myself back in my bed once more, I would instinctively reach out and touch the wall of my bedroom. If I could feel the hard plaster of the wall on my fingers then I knew I was back to full consciousness and more importantly safe from the advances of this killer. But, if I couldn't feel the wall…

One night, during an attack, I awoke to find a large Native American sitting at the end of my bed. This man was much bigger and more intimidating than my usual attacker, yet for some reason I wasn't afraid of this man and I felt that I could trust him. I would later discover that this was indeed my spirit guide and he was protecting me from negative energy forces.

My parents were aware of my frequent nightmares but they would always say that it was just bad dreams and that every child suffered from them. Somehow, I knew that this wasn't true but as time wore on I decided that my only salvation was to endure these dreams the best way I could – after all, I never was physically harmed, thankfully waking up just in time.

In adulthood, the dreams became less frequent and thankfully less troublesome. Even my wife, Anne, would get used to waking up suddenly and hearing me shouting out at the mad knifeman and we would usually just laugh about it afterwards. Then, one night, Anne unexpectedly saw the man standing over me about to pounce, just as I was about to shout out to break free from the nightmare. Incredibly, she described the man exactly as I had always seen him, even though she initially thought that it was actually me standing next to my bed.

Many years later, my son Dylan witnessed the man running into my bedroom as he was being chased by another much bigger man. The next morning, Dylan described the knifeman exactly as Anne and I had previously recalled. His description of the chasing man also fitted that of my spirit guide. These occurrences convinced me that I wasn't just dreaming. There had to be some form of realism when other people had witnessed the exact same figures as I had. I needed to investigate this further and find out more about the man with the knife. My eventual discovery of the truth would completely shock me to the core. Additionally, I would also uncover the answers to so many questions about my life here on Earth, and beyond, that had intrigued me throughout my spiritual journey – answers that were so obvious that I couldn't believe it took me so long to find them.

I have always been fascinated by Past Life Regression and it was the study of my own past lives that finally brought me to the answers that I so craved to find. Now, what I am about to tell you is relevant to my own life and my discovery was only procured to make sense of my own path through eternal life. Whether your life echoes the path of mine is totally up to you.

The worst experience of my current life, by some considerable distance, occurred after returning to full consciousness from a self-induced past life regression session. The realisation that I had murdered and mutilated several people in Australia during the 1850's was bad enough, but the experience felt so real to me that for around thirty minutes afterwards I contemplated ending my own life due to the immense emotional turmoil that I was left with. It's difficult to describe the intolerable feelings that I suffered directly afterwards but I can honestly say that I never want to feel that way ever again. The intense feelings of shame, guilt and remorse are beyond anything that you could ever possibly imagine.

Not surprisingly, I had many questions to ask my spirit guides concerning this horrific ordeal, but they were extremely vague with any answers. I now know that the reason for this is that we must endure many life changing experiences before we can fully appreciate the power of eternal living. Spirit guides may well have all the answers but they are only ever our teachers and we shouldn't expect to be given the correct answers to any examination we ever sit. Also, any information brought forward by my guides in relation to choices that I make throughout my existence could theoretically affect any future choices made by me – and that level of interference would not be permissible in any capacity.

I do believe that the emotional turmoil that I underwent after the regression session was just a stark reminder of what I would have endured after passing to spirit from that life in the 1850's. I suppose the most important thing that I can take from a life that was so violent and disturbing is the fact that when the time came to judge myself there was no escaping from it and I will forever be reminded of my actions – even after returning to the physical world once more. More importantly, I know that I would be willing to do absolutely anything to escape from the most horrendous feeling imaginable.

But where do the persistent nightmares with the mad knifeman fit into all of this? Could there be a connection between the two? After all, if I had committed unspeakable crimes against poor innocent Australians, would I not expect to be reminded of those crimes on a daily basis? Incredibly, I would soon discover that there was no connection whatsoever between them, and the reason for this opened up a whole Universe of questions and answers, which would eventually explain the functionality behind the evolution of my own eternal life.

I've always been fascinated by Scottish castles and the turbulent history enriched within each of the battle-stained stone walls. On many occasions when visiting them, I have imagined what it would have been like having to defend against invaders, intent on reaping and pillaging their way through anything that stood in their way. Intriguingly, I never imagined myself being part of an army that was attacking a castle – instead, I was always the man who led the defence against an attack, trying to stem a force that was much greater in number and armament. I can only presume that this is why I enjoyed watching films like The Alamo and Zulu, where courageous men fought to defend their fortresses against seemingly impossible odds.

One of my favourite areas to visit in Scotland is Perthshire, and as this beautiful area was once the heartland of Scottish nobility, there are many historical venues to visit – one of which is Blair Castle near the beautiful village of Blair Atholl. As a young man, I visited this place with my family – ironically, many years before I became involved with the spirit world. I can still vividly recall my experience...

Looking out through the large windows of the castle to the land spread out below, I started to visualise large groups of soldiers preparing to fire upon the defenders of the castle. Instinctively, I began to order the men beside me to defend each window from attack and to make sure that they received enough ammunition to fire back at the invaders. I could hear lots of shouting from outside as the assailants prepared for attack and everyone around me frantically took up position.

Then, suddenly, my vision came back into focus and I was back in the present day. Normally when this kind of odd experience occurs, I will gaze out to the scene of the battle and the landscape will look completely different, further enforcing to my consciousness that I had just experienced some form of unrelated abreaction. However, on this occasion, to my astonishment, the landscape seemed very similar in proportion – almost as if I had just leapt forward in time from the exact same location. A shiver ran down my spine as I surveyed my surroundings, both inside and outside of the castle, and I came to the conclusion that I must surely have been here before – a déjà vu moment. Not only that, it felt like I had never really left this place.

Around one hundred miles north of this castle, there is a historical site where a great battle took place. The battle of Culloden was fought during the Jacobean uprising and when I visited this site I instinctively felt that I had died in this battle. The same feelings of déjà vu that I experienced in the castle were prevalent here, although this time I felt strangely comforted from a wave of serene calmness that suggested closure, as opposed to the expected feelings of mass anxiety and trauma.

My visit to the castle affected me greatly for some time afterwards. I could not find a reason as to why this would be other than the presumption that my nightmares were connected in some way. After all, the appearance and the attire of my attacker somewhat fitted the description of a soldier from this time period. There was also the fact that my nightmares became more frequent after the visit to the castle. It almost felt like I had reopened old wounds and rediscovered the true fear behind my past.

I eventually came to the fairly obvious conclusion that I had been a defender of Blair Castle in charge of many men and had been stabbed through the heart by one of the leaders of the opposing army once the castle walls had been breached. It made perfect sense to me. I was just continually reliving the experience in my subconscious and the fear associated with this death had clearly remained with me throughout my present physical life.

Once I had accepted these events had taken place, I rather hoped that the nightmares would finally end – but they didn't. Even after I began to work with the spirit world through mediumship and spiritual writing, the nightmares continued, despite my spirit guides continually offering me protection during my sleep.

The good thing about performing past life regressions in the 21st century is that there is so much historical information available nowadays - quite literally at your fingertips. The internet is awash with both chronological facts and theoretical beliefs from as far back as the first recorded words. Therefore, I naively believed that it would be really easy to find evidence of my existence in both of these time periods due to the severity of my crimes in Australia and the fact that the attack on Blair Castle was the last known siege to have ever taken place in this country.

Eventually, after trawling through numerous accounts of murderous savagery in nineteenth century Australia, I found a strong connection between a man who was executed for murdering a mother and daughter in their own home.

An Australian author had collated a record of many early serial killers and his account of this crime and timeframe matched my own recollection. He also stated that the murderer initially hailed from Scotland, having been transported to Australia as a petty thief. The only variance seemed to be that I visualised committing my crimes at the back of a shop and not in a woman's home. However, the author had researched this case further and discovered that the local police suspected that the killer may also have been responsible for numerous deaths in another town, several months before, which had remained unsolved. Apparently, these murders of a similar ilk were committed in the back of a shop. Of course, there was no way of connecting those crimes forensically in the 1850's and the fact that the killer was eventually hanged was enough to satisfy local magistrates that no further investigations were necessary.

I have no doubt in my mind that I was the perpetrator of these crimes. It's impossible to find absolute proof but there are times in your life when you are just so absolutely sure of something that it really couldn't be considered coincidental. This truly was a horrific period of my eternal life that I could not and should not ever forget. All that remains with me is the fact that I fully accept what I did and I also recognise the consequences to the other lives that I destroyed.

But what answers did I find from this ordeal? I believe that the only thing I can actually take from it is the fact that if someone is fortunate to escape capture after committing any heinous crime in this physical world, then what's waiting for them in the next dimension is the most intense self-torture imaginable. I can only hope that this is of some comfort to anyone who is still in torment due to their loved one's murderer not being brought to justice in the physical world.

The historical events surrounding my past life as a Jacobean soldier during the 18th century should have been much easier to source – but they weren't. In fact, there were so many holes in this personal investigation that on many occasions I felt that I could not possibly have been at this particular place in time.

These were the facts that I felt were true;

1. I was a Jacobite fighting against the Government soldiers
2. I died at the battle of Culloden
3. My constant nightmares focussed on a murder committed within Blair Castle.

Conversely, history states that it was actually the Jacobites who laid siege to the castle and not the Government soldiers loyal to the Crown. Furthermore, why was I continually witnessing my own murder in the castle if I strongly believed that I died a short time later at Culloden? Last, but certainly not least – how could I be tormented by an event that resulted in my own death, rather than a crime committed by myself?

These questions continually swirled around my mind and I constantly asked my spirit guides to point me in the right direction, and finally, after many deep trance meditations, I began to piece together the jigsaw, and it all centred on my wife's initial feeling about the man she saw standing next to my bed. My findings were as follow…

In this physical world, there is a widely held view that eternal living focusses on a concept of many different physical existences and identities, developed through centuries of diverse cultural habitats. In other words, we all live and die, before returning in a new guise - completely oblivious to how our previous existence panned out. Except, of course, when we choose to scrutinise our subconscious mind and discover traces of past lives and the traumatic memories associated with them. But surely they're all in the past, am I not correct? The answer I eventually uncovered was an emphatic 'no'.

I discovered that there is only ever the one existence. It is only ever our physical bodies that change. Whatever has taken place in a past physical existence is a result of actions borne from our subconscious mind – and that subconscious mind is the same one that you retain throughout eternity. In other words – I am still the same soul who terrorised those poor Australians – maybe not in flesh and blood – but totally in thought and mind, which explains why I felt so bad after recalling my actions through regression.

In conclusion, I can now clearly see why my present physical existence is closely centred on preserving all life forms and appreciating them in whatever capacity they exist in. My experience in Australia has taught me about the importance of allowing people to flourish rather than hinder their existence through my own weaknesses. In addition, I have found that I must respect all life in its entirety, even though I'm fully aware that death is not permanent and any crimes committed against humanity can eventually be redressed, however traumatic the resulting circumstances.

With this discovery in mind, I approached the events of the Jacobean era with the exact same analogy – that those events took place in my eternal lifetime, the memories of which still adversely affected me due to the result of my own thoughts and actions. Nevertheless, many holes still remained unfilled. Why was I being tormented by the actions of another malevolent soul who was intent on murdering me? My self-discovery was about to take another significant twist.

When I wrote the book "New Mediumship" in 2012, I discovered the reason why we occasionally witness apparitions or ghosts, and why this is such a rare occurrence. My guides taught me that when we return to the spirit world after physical death there is a brief period where we have the opportunity to self-evaluate all actions resulting from that journey to the physical world. Typically, after realising that life is indeed eternal and that the physical world has little bearing on the virtues of eternal living, most souls readily accept any recommendations brought forward by their spirit guides in relation to further evolving their existence. However, there are always one or two exceptions, where certain souls just cannot accept that their actions in the physical life that's just ended were morally unjust, with the result that further examination of these events must now take place so that they will eventually realise the error of their ways.

What transpires next is a thought-based journey back to the source of any troubling issues, and it's always accompanied by your main spirit guide. If this does not bring closure and acceptance to these events then the journey must be continually repeated, which can develop into a continuous energy loop travelling between both dimensions.

Very occasionally, if you were to visit the scene of one of these continuous loops then you might just catch a glimpse of a soul retracing the steps that led to the event which has caused their emotional turmoil – almost like watching a video recording of the actual event. My guides informed me that when people believe they have seen a ghost, they have in fact just momentarily witnessed a small segment of one of these loops. It is worth noting that souls caught up in interdimensional loops are not aware of any corporeal elements surrounding them during these journeys, which explains why there are never any physical interactions between human beings and the ghosts that they witness.

I was further advised by my guides that if a soul continually refuses to accept the responsibilities associated with a previous physical life experience, even after continuously reviewing the evidence through an interdimensional loop, then they will be offered the opportunity to reincarnate to a physical life once again in order to redress the issues there, albeit in a different capacity. Here, they will be given the chance to live their life in a more fulfilling fashion, which should hopefully allow the soul to realise where they have went wrong with their beliefs or actions. As a reminder though, the recurring loop will continue in their subconscious mind, taking the soul back to the point of discretion – until all the pieces of the jigsaw slowly fit into place.

This is where my own journey became extremely interesting. I discovered that my recurring nightmares were in fact my subconscious mind retracing a loop which opened up after my death at Culloden. This loop would subsequently fail to be addressed effectively during my later life in Australia, even though my crimes committed there must have surely eclipsed whatever took place as a Jacobite soldier.

On reflection, it soon became obvious to me that I had indeed fully accepted my responsibility for the dreadful crimes in Australia, but whatever had taken place at Blair Castle remained dormant in my mind - the reason for this remained a mystery.

Incredibly, everything then suddenly clicked into place, and I couldn't believe how I had missed the solution to the puzzle. Eventually, my intuition confirmed to me that I had indeed been a Jacobite soldier during the siege at Blair Castle, and furthermore, had later died at Culloden as initially suspected. Moreover, I found out that my continuous nightmares were actually an interdimensional loop which took me to Blair Castle where I would witness a callous murder taking place. The mysterious man with long, black hair and beard would thrust his knife deep into the heart of his victim, killing him callously. As I relived this crime over and over again in my mind, I further discovered that this loop would occasionally be witnessed by those in the physical world, just catching a tiny glimpse before the murderer disappeared… until the next time.

It intrigued me that someone else could witness this murder taking place in my timeless loop, believing that they had just witnessed a ghost. I also wondered if Anne thought she had witnessed a ghost when she saw a figure standing beside my bed during one of my nightmares, and that's when the penny finally dropped. If I was stuck in a loop where I was struggling to come to terms with something that I had done wrong then it could surely only mean one thing – I was… in fact… the murderer!

How could I have missed the facts?

1. Anne initially thought that the man standing over my bed was in fact me.
2. My son witnessed this man and my spirit guide running into my bedroom together.
3. The Jacobite's were the attackers at the siege of Blair Castle – not the defenders.
4. Finally, deep down I knew that my fear associated with this crime was not a fear of dying, but rather a fear of accepting responsibility for my own actions.

It had finally dawned on me that the perpetrator of this crime was actually myself, the reality at last sinking in that for all those years, when I believed that I was being haunted by a knife-wielding murderer, that in actual fact, I was being haunted… by myself!

I further realised that I was reliving this crime through the eyes of the victim in order for me to appreciate the true extent of my actions. History records that the Jacobean War was fought at a time when many families or close friends fought on either side, often depending on where their allegiances lay. This conflict was more of a civil war than a war between nations and as a result many siblings or close relatives were killed by members of their own family. It is also worth noting that the Jacobites did not eventually capture the castle, instead leaving the scene to fight at Culloden. Nonetheless, there would almost certainly have been raids on the castle during the siege and lives would have been lost on both sides.

I do not know the identity of either myself or the person I murdered at the castle, but I strongly suspect that it was a member of my close family. I also believe that this is the main reason why I failed to acknowledge the error of my ways when the time came to evaluate my actions in this life.

Of course, I may just be imagining this whole episode in my eternal life. After all, without physical evidence I cannot prove to you or indeed myself that I did commit this crime, never mind relive it every other week or so in my subconscious mind. All I can state is that when I communicated with my guide and asked for confirmation, I was furnished with the same sense of serene calmness that was with me during my visit to Culloden. It also felt like a huge weight had suddenly been lifted off my shoulders.

Since this remarkable discovery, almost a year ago, I have not experienced any further visits from the knifeman, and my sleep pattern has never been smoother now that my loop has been discovered, analysed and suitably acknowledged. I know I will eventually meet the person from this loop soon enough and I hope a suitable resolution for both parties can be agreed – both of our soul's evolving journeys now depend on it.

This is my story; yours may be similar or completely different. I hope you may find a way of breaking free from whatever is holding you back. After all, we are but one small part of the evolution of eternal life.

CONCLUSION: SEARCHING FOR WAILUA FALLS

Wailua Falls in the Hawaiian Islands is often regarded as one of the most beautiful places on Earth. You may not have visited this place personally but you've probably seen it on television – it was featured on the opening scenes of the iconic seventies series "Fantasy Island" as well as featuring on many film sets.

The beauty of this idyllic place is its natural surroundings – lush greenery embedded within the most wonderful double waterfall, cascading gently downwards to a pool of utter tranquillity.

Visually, this place is absolutely stunning, and despite having being visited by millions of people from all over the world, it remains to this day, unspoiled by human hands. Unlike Niagra Falls, there is no need for any commercial outlets here, since this is somewhere that human beings come to just forget themselves and forget everything that may be blighting their lives. For here you can find a place where all but the simplest of things can make your heart gently flutter and your mind effortlessly unwind to the point of blissful harmony.

Alas, the huge financial cost of visiting this wondrous island may be just too much for most people, meaning that this visual paradise will remain all but a pipedream in your head. Nevertheless, you can but dream that one day this fantasy may become a reality.

Legend suggests that beauty always lies in the eyes of the beholder – from the first time you open your eyes to the world, to the last time you wave goodbye to family and friends. Life is only ever as beautiful as you want it to be. It is all but the contrast in your mind that determines such a beauty, through either redeeming or contemptuous eyes. However, for every barren, grey sky that enters your world, a vision of Wailua Falls beckons around every corner.

You may search and search for this tropical paradise in your mind, dismissing everything that willingly presents itself, before eventually realising that it's already right there in front of your eyes – where it has always been, conceivably undetected through morbid and delusional thinking.

When I initially arrived back in this big, bad, physical planet that we all presently seem to hate so much, I distinctly remember falling gently down through my very own Wailua Falls before softly landing on my heels. I now know that when I return to the next step of my eternal journey that I will find myself back at the glorious waterfall – where it all began, hoping that my voyage home will be as smooth as my first steps here.

We are now aware that, for many of us, the main purpose of any visit back to this physical planet is to break free from the restraints of our self-engineered interdimensional loop. We also know that this loop can affect our state of mind to such an extent that we may find ourselves enduring constant nightmares, with an inability to escape free from them. Furthermore, if we remain caught in this timeless loop then our lives cannot continue to evolve in a more productive and purposeful fashion. In many ways, we remain stifled by senseless ordeals.

Thankfully, we now know that we have the ability to break free from these endless chains of thought that continually hold us back. If we can only change our ways of understanding life and more importantly, fully accepting of whatever life throws at us, then we can begin to appreciate whatever circumstances have caused us to question our existence in this or any other dimension.

But, of course, it's never that easy, is it? We shouldn't expect to build a palatial ornament in our mind without first creating the tools to do it. We shouldn't expect to find love in other people without first loving ourselves, nor look for the beauty of Wailua Falls before searching for inner beauty.

Life is eternal and the soul that returns to this Earth is still the same soul that previously left here. You cannot change who you are but you can change the way you feel about someone, something, or, just as importantly, the way you feel about yourself. To achieve this you must break down all the barriers that you initially created around your mundane thoughts and actions. The world around you will continually test you so that you can measure your ability to compromise and rejuvenate your soul and all other souls within your chosen path. Only then will you be truly ready to address the issues in your loop.

Life in the physical world is but an opportunity to redress any imbalances in your eternal life – indeed an opportunity to kick-start your endless journey. Your spiritual passport contains everything that you need for a safe journey home. It is worth remembering that you could live for a hundred years on Earth and still not earn every appropriate stamp on your passport. Conversely, you could conceivably take just one solitary breath and attain everything that you initially set out to achieve. It's not how long you live on Earth that's important – it's how well you live.

In my own case, I needed to readdress everything that had created the monster within me. In hindsight, this was a loop that needed a lot of work to break free from. Sometimes, there lies a particular failure that is often much greater than the sum of any achievements.

Every one of us is different in so many ways, so finding and dissecting all of our individual issues takes great patience and strength of mind. Only once all the pieces are laid out on the table can you begin to piece together the forgotten puzzle.

We are now well aware of the importance of maintaining a healthy balanced eternal existence, whether in this physical life or the next stage of our continually evolving journey home. The ten guidelines that we have discussed will remind us of everything that is important in life. However, if after returning to the spirit dimension we were to find ourselves in an interdimensional loop, then we can still use these important guidelines to free ourselves from the loop, before discovering the hidden delights of Wailua Falls all over again.

My life is far from perfect

When we find ourselves in a timeless loop of relapsing thoughts then we should always look upon the quest to free ourselves from this process as a task worth embracing with a strong positive mind frame. As we have previously discovered, perfection is a state of being that is way beyond anything that we could ever imagine. In a world as vast as this is, there is so much still to discover that we cannot conceivably presume that our lives are complete, with no need to improve on anything.

Timeless energy loops are simply a reminder of this fact. We cannot profess to self-completion when all around us is continually changing and evolving. It is imperative that we mirror these fluctuations in eternal life so that anything holding us back will open up to allow additional freedom of choice and inspiration. These new inspired choices will almost certainly herald further imperfections in any future self-evaluations, but we should always embrace every one of them as only then can we learn more about ourselves.

You must never look upon any loop as a failure in life – that way of thinking will only cause further regression and stifle your evolving life. Look upon this route as just a learning curve and I promise you that when you emerge from this process you won't feel a hint of perfection in any manner – rather a small sense of satisfaction and accomplishment – earned through a path of solid realisation.

"The humblest of souls will always view imperfections as the perfect way to remain humble. Knowledge is the gateway to our soul. With nothing left to learn we shall drift continuously in endless loops of self-absorption, only breaking free once the choice to expand one's consciousness becomes the considered elucidation."

I am willing to forgive myself as well as others

The importance of forgiveness in any society is of paramount importance to any individual's development. It may sound easy to forgive someone for their thoughts or actions, but it's vitally important that you first understand why they chose to cause you emotional distress. Likewise, if you were to ask forgiveness from another person, then you should present to them explanations as to why you acted this way. In many cases, we must fully open up our souls to each other and hope that conditioned reasoning will prevail to allow us to move on with our eternal living.

The existence of any interdimensional loop will more often than not contain an element of unforgiving circumstances. In my own case, I could not see that I had in fact committed a crime rather than be the victim, as first thought. My inability to comprehend the malevolent nature of the event in the spirit dimension had clouded my judgement, thus leaving me lost in the physical world without true understanding of the depth of my situation.

In truth, I wasn't being haunted by a callous murderer, but by my own inability to accept my part in the conflict. In hindsight, my actions as a serial killer in a subsequent incarnation led me to believe that this was the only redemption that needed to be accountable for, even though my constant nightmares never ever centred on this particular existence.

Forgiveness in the physical world can sometimes help us to appreciate and accept the love and compassion that widely exists amongst human beings, but it is in the ethereal world that awaits us where forgiveness becomes an absolute necessity if we are to evolve our eternal existence.

I have now discovered the reality of my constant nightmares and accepted that they were self-instigated by me. My life in the physical world can now progress with a heightened sense of positivity and serenity. However, it won't be until I return to the spirit dimension before I can reconnect with the soul that I killed and offer my forgiveness in a manner that both of us now accept as spiritually harmonious. Only then, can my passport be fully stamped accordingly, and my eternal existence set free from the restraints of the torturous loop.

My heart skips a beat at the end of the film "It's a Wonderful Life"

It's currently 03:30 in the morning of the 14th July 2020. Only a few days ago, I felt a sharp pain in my lower back whilst attempting to lift a heavy bag of garden stone chips. Unbeknown to me at the time, this rather trivial injury would prevent me from comfortably sitting upright for the next couple of days, thus preventing me from writing this section of the book.

Alas, just a few hours ago, I felt my intuition prompt me to recommence writing as my spirit friends were primed for connecting with me. Hence, my seating position was set as best as I thought possible and a strong cup of coffee was hastily prepared for the sleepless journey ahead.

The reality is that my back is still painful, yet manageable to the extent that enduring physical pain is something that I know should be embraced rather than continually frowned upon. I was reminded of this fact only a few moments ago when my son telephoned me. He said that he couldn't sleep and was worried about my injury, suggesting that perhaps I should just rest until the injury was fully healed. We had actually discussed this matter earlier in the day when I was complaining about the constant pain from bending down to pick up items that I shouldn't have dropped in the first place.

I knew then that he was feeling my pain – not physically of course, but intuitively. Because, believe it or not, souls that are connected in this way will always sense when something is not quite right within the soul family – be it major trauma or just a simple muscle injury. In fact, in some way it's almost impossible to ignore the emotional distress felt by a member of any soul group.

Nowadays, the stark reality is that many of us struggle to look after family members who are unable to properly look after themselves, in many different capacities, and this can place a huge physical and emotional burden on our shoulders. At times, it will almost feel like we are making huge sacrifices for the welfare of our soul families and this seemingly never-ending loop can become a huge test of any individual's character.

Life, as we are constantly reminded, is not always a bed of roses laid out at our feet. Often we are tested to see if lessons truly are learned from past indifferences. The best way to atone for any previous errors of judgement is to find yourself in a similar environment where you will have the opportunity to enhance a soul group, rather than choose a path of self-indulgence. Not straying from this path is the greatest test that any soul will ever endure in a physical context.

I thanked my son for contacting me and asking about my welfare. I informed him that my back was much better, even though I will almost certainly struggle to stand up straight after finishing these words. The point being that he was concerned for my welfare – and that he cared deeply about my physical and emotional health. In truth, he was looking out for me – as I would automatically do for him.

Incredibly, the fact that my son expressed compassion for my wellbeing actually removed the pain from the strained muscles in my back, albeit temporarily. Having someone to look out for you is a precious commodity that offers many healing qualities. Sometimes you don't need to watch a classic Hollywood movie for your heart to skip a beat. I bid you a good night…

The only wealth that I truly need is knowledge

The constant battle with materialism is by far the most challenging aspect of any soul's journey within this physical world. The prospect of having a lifestyle enriched by luxurious products and friends in so-called high places can catapult one's ego to the point of no return. Yet, once a soul that's been bitten by the materialistic bug returns to the spirit world then they are shocked to find that their life has actually been stifled by their choices, since there is no place for such self-indulgence in the spirit dimension.

I have always been advised by my guides that living a life of extreme luxury can often be more difficult to atone for than a life of violence or even murder when we return home. The reason being that it is easy to see where you went wrong if you murdered another soul, but discovering that the wealth that you built up during your physical life has now created such disharmony from within yourself is always going to be difficult to comprehend.

Every single soul that travels to the physical world has to endure a part of their life that is surrounded by materialistic opportunities. This is simply because it is part of our training – we need to understand that greed and power are totally redundant in a non-physical environment and the only way to fully understand this is to become a victim of its tenure.

I have been reliably informed that my own eternal life became a victim of extreme materialism during the Jacobean War. I was in fact a wealthy landowner and statesman and I betrayed my own family for greed and power. I can only speculate that this is one of the main reasons as to why I found it difficult to atone for this period of my life and ended up in the debilitating loop.

When the motive to murder someone is for materialistic gain then there is never any comeback once you review the journey that's just ended. My exploits in Australia may have been horrific but the motive here was entirely different and in this instance relatively easy to atone for in comparison.

Wealth in any form should always be measured by what good it can do for you. If it's to benefit or boost your ego then it should be avoided. However, we must remember that we are here to learn about life in a different fashion from what we are used to in the spirit world. Therefore if we do decide to better ourselves through a lifestyle of exuberance then it is vital that we do so to enjoy the experience, before sharing it with others who have still to understand the probable implications of these choices.

It is also important to understand that if materialism in this world did not exist then we would be living in a perfect world – almost identical to the spirit world. But what would be the fun in that? We are here to learn about the so-called bad side of life every bit as much as the good side, so embrace the stimulating effects of materialism and all that it can throw at you. Only then, when you come out the other side, will you be able to fully appreciate the beauty of souls who prefer to share all that they have with no expectations in return.

Every soul has the ability to share love

Love is much more than just a four letter word that implies affection between souls. In the spirit dimension, love is the energy force that connects souls to a common cause. In essence, this connection becomes almost automatic in structure, meaning that every soul will find in some shape or form a common link to love, regardless of the circumstances that brought them back to the spirit dimension.

This process defines every soul in a way that becomes symptomatic of everyday life in the spirit world. The only deflection from this procedure occurs when the detrimental effects of any loop causes sufficient interference to an individual's thought process. At this point, souls should consider their options to ensure that their development is not stunted by a failure to accept that love is present in their thoughts.

Love is never absent in any life development, either in the physical or spiritual planes. Finding love from within yourself in the realms of the physical world can aid your task of breaking free from any restrictive loop. Then, you can take this experience home to your spiritual family and share the knowledge that you attain in the process. This knowledge will in turn help members of your spiritual family to aid their own development should they then choose to visit the physical world.

Loving someone in the physical world, no matter how brief that may be, is an experience worth coming here for. Everything else that affects our stay here is all but a by-product of love. The experience of sharing love with one and other is something that expands a soul's consciousness beyond anything else.

When we lose a loved one in the physical world then the heartache of this loss can sometimes be beyond any pain imaginable to the human spirit. However, once reunited in the spirit world, the power of love between lost souls will return unequivocally.

I am the creator of all that is truthful

There is no escaping from the absolute truth when finding one's self within the confines of a timeless loop. Furthermore, it is extremely important that we should realise the implications of denying the ownership of one's actions once any divergence opens up between souls.

The mainstay of truthfulness within the spirit dimension is the fact that absolute honesty must always be reciprocated. If one soul's version of events differs from another then truth cannot exist between these two souls, regardless of the circumstances. The existence of telepathic thought process will always ensure that spirit people are incapable of lying, thus sending a deceitful soul back to the place where any discrepancy occurred – which will either cause a timeless loop to commence or just continue unabated.

Rather surprisingly, truth is not *the* moral compass for a salubrious existence in the spirit dimension; rather it is simply an influential factor for enabling harmonious agreement within the confines of any soul group. Knowledge is the key element for soul evolution and truth is actually just part of the fuel that keeps this engine continually running. To deny yourself the truth will only temporarily put the brakes on your endless journey, but once acknowledged, truth will reignite any voyage back to the stage that it has always been at, leaving you with a feeling that you have improved your life skills and not regressed back the way.

The most daunting part of this process is that you may believe that you are true to yourself, yet still find yourself unable to break free from your loop. The extreme emotions that are often felt in a loop will sometimes make any soul unwilling to accept the turbulent nature of the event that took place back on Earth. By examining the circumstances surrounding the event, it is often found that the non-existence of truth between souls has heavily influenced the resulting actions, creating a state of confusion that is hugely difficult to comprehend.

In my own loop created after my Jacobean incarnation, I truly believed that I was betrayed and murdered by a member of my family because of my loyalties to others. Unfortunately, my family member disagreed with this explanation and the resultant disharmony created the loop, since truth cannot exist unless it's reciprocated. The confusing aspects of this crime eventually made me believe that I was in fact the victim rather than the murderer. Ultimately, I had to look outside of the loop and journey through new physical incarnations in order to finally find a connection with the soul that I had in fact murdered, before rediscovering the true events of that existence.

Now, due to the fact that I have discovered that I was the perpetrator of this crime and not the victim as first thought, truth finally exists between us and our journeys can resume in earnest, yet there is still the small matter of us both accepting the events and circumstances that transpired during that period. Only then will we both be able to use truth to furnish greater knowledge of our lives and relay these facts to others on similar life paths.

In conclusion, truthfulness is the fuel that propels endless journeys, whereas an unwillingness to accept the truth will send us spiralling into interdimensional loops. You can always stay true to yourself, but it is more vital that you exude truth with accepting souls.

I am willing to accept any failures as a success

Accepting all of your failures in a physical life is without doubt the prime criteria for ensuring a smooth and successful transition into a permanent residence within the spirit dimension. In our material world we are constantly reminded by the pillars of society that success in life is always guaranteed by working harder and smarter than your competitor in a battle of self-indulgent willpower. Ironically, it is from this specific form of human behaviour that the vast majority of interdimensional loops are then created.

If a soul was to return to the spirit dimension after having successfully created a huge amount of personal wealth, and was then informed by their spiritual elders that their materialistic lifestyle had stifled the objectives that had initially been set out for them, then it is understandable that a degree of confusion would often prevail. It would then become a matter of digesting all of the choices made before deciding if they could fully accept the manner in which life should really be judged – not by status, but by experiences, whether good or bad.

Loops can never be breached if all terms and conditions cannot be accepted. Therefore, it is imperative that all perceived failures are looked upon with the same degree of importance as any perceived accomplishments.

Never has there has been a soul that has ascended successfully to a permanent residence within the Free Dimension who truly believes their self to have been cast from a faultless mind.

The above quotation came directly from a spirit consciousness. It is interesting to note the use of the term Free Dimension. This is the first time that I have ever heard this term and it personally resonates well with me. I will now choose to use this term instead of Spirit Dimension. It is also worth noting the important message behind this quote – in essence it is saying that it is impossible to migrate back to the Free Dimension unless we believe and accept that we have made mistakes, or harvested regrets. Once this has been achieved then we will be able to toast success in its truest form.

I am no more impressive than the humblest hobo

Once we arrive back at the Free Dimension and discover that personal status is only ever quantified as a mark of belonging to groups of like-minded souls, rather than a measure of fervent competition between souls, we may begin to appreciate the importance of remaining humble in all forms of differing opinions. Therefore, finding ourselves in a timeless loop due to a conflict of interests with another soul will undoubtedly highlight indifferences in the way we continually view the precise circumstances of any disagreements.

For example, in my own loop I saw myself as the poor victim of a heinous crime by a powerful individual, whereas in reality it was actually me who was the more affluent and influential person. Moreover, the main reason that I chose to kill my family member was to ensure that my affluence remained intact.

It is easy to express regret to another soul for taking their life, but first you must always lay out the reasons why you chose to act this way before showing that you now understand that those circumstances were flawed in conception. The spiritual guidelines that we have already discussed will aid this task and help you in any re-evaluation, but sometimes we may have to look further afield just to fit in all the missing pieces.

We will always be continually tested in any subsequent physical incarnation. In my own case, I am now fully aware that all people on this planet should be treated as equals in every aspect of life, regardless of their actions, choices, lifestyle or material wealth. However, it has taken me fifty physical years to finally come to this conclusion, in addition to at least one, possibly more, post-Jacobean incarnations.

We must never underestimate the circumstances surrounding the cause of any loop that's been self-created. Not everything in life is black and white. Don't look for flaws in others until you discover and deal with your own. Only then will you find a true sense of belonging in the most humbling of worlds.

I must heal myself before attempting to heal others

To heal one's self in the Free Dimension is to simply become more aware of yourself and your surroundings. There is no need for meditation or relaxation techniques as your consciousness moves at the same flow as everyone else in your soul group. You cannot feel physical pain in the Free Dimension and you will not be hampered by negative emotions as neither exists once you have established a permanent residence in a purely conscious environment.

However, if your transition to the Free Dimension has been hindered by regretful actions from your just ended physical incarnation, then the repercussions will resonate with your spiritual lifestyle and this must be addressed in whatever capacity possible. In other words, you will almost certainly be affected by extreme emotional heartache and you must do everything in your power to rectify this as you reverberate between both dimensions.

Grief is the main cause of any hurt left behind and this is why spirit people seek out the skills of spirit mediums, hoping that a few words of comfort will aid the grieving process of their loved ones so that they can resume their own life journey in a positive fashion. In most cases it does, but on rare occasions, for whatever reason, there is a breakdown in awareness – and inevitably a loop is created.

Of course, there are other more serious reasons as to why pain or emotional turmoil has been created by your passing, thus the danger of a loop being created is much higher.

Throughout every ounce of your existence in either the physical or spiritual worlds you will always have the opportunity to seek guidance from your spiritual elders and guides. They can and will point you towards a positive outcome but it is up to you to choose this option, even if sometimes you can't see the wood for the trees.

The most important aspect of any reconciliatory action is to become aware of all the surrounding circumstances. In my own case, I naively believed that I was the victim rather than the killer. Sometimes you need to walk in the footsteps of others to appreciate their ways and beliefs. If this can be achieved then you will be well on your way to healing yourself from all forms of self-doubt and lack of understanding. In this case, healing yourself will undoubtedly heal others.

A question that I am regularly asked is "After passing to spirit, why do some souls choose to return to the physical dimension and yet others choose to remain there?" The answer is incredibly straightforward – In a pain free, mindfully rewarding world you will never ever wish to leave there. In contrast, if you find yourself caught in an interdimensional loop, where emotional pain and suffering remain a hindrance to your well-being, then you will do absolutely everything you can to break free and finally gain perpetual residence in the Free Dimension.

I am but one small part of the Evolution of Eternal Life

Each night that you settle your weary head down against the soft cotton pillow in your bed, you will very rarely ever think about the incredible journey that you are about to embark on. You may have just experienced a highly traumatic, or perhaps an extremely stimulating day, that still plays heavily on your mind - and naturally your thoughts will travel back and forth between the events of the day just passed and the events that you perceive may transpire tomorrow, before your subconscious mind slowly takes you deeper down into an immense world of dreams.

Some of the greatest minds of our past have invariably attempted to analyse the dream world and make common sense of it, but many have failed miserably. The psychological work of Sigmund Freud is legendary in its in-depth analysis, scrutinising the power of the human brain in a lifetime of behavioural discovery – the like of which has never been replicated even today. But, his analysis of the dream state in humans is deeply flawed since his refusal to believe in the existence of life after physical death left his tool bag short of many spanners.

His colleague however, fared far better in this field. Carl Jung believed in a collective unconscious that existed in not only this life but possibly in another dimension. Alas, his theories were dismissed by Freud and all others in his profession, rather ironically at a time when many wealthy Victorians were actively attempting to contact "the dead" through séances. Jung could not provide valid evidence of this fact and the conclusion remained that dreams are only abreactions of the subconscious part of the brain – imaginative thoughts created when the body is relaxed and the brain is left to wander aimlessly through clouds of disjointed emotions.

When you fall asleep tonight your brain will actually behave like a television set that has been left on standby, with only a small amount of power needed to function. The brain will only resume full power when the subconscious mind intentionally switches it back on - either because it is time for you to wake up due to scheduled commitments – or your energy has somehow been traumatised and the safety net of the physical world will relieve any emotional distress. In summary – your subconscious mind is completely separate from your brain; it has complete control and will direct every thought appropriately.

It normally takes us over two physical hours to reach that part of our mind that generates full dream capacity. This is when we arrive at – wait for it – the Free Dimension. Yes, that's correct – we travel into the world of spirits every night. Physicists for hundreds of years have tried to find the mystical Fifth Dimension, where the other four dimensions become obsolete and space-time relativity is turned on its head, and all along they can find this place every single night of their physical lives. The fifth dimension is …the Free Dimension.

It is very rare that any of us ever remember our dreams after waking up. If we did, then we would also remember our past lives more vividly. The importance of our nightly journey to the Free Dimension is extremely low in our pursuit of eternal enlightenment. The main purpose of such adventures is to simply relax our bodies and mind so that we may function satisfactorily in the next physical day. Now here comes the interesting part. Whereas our nightly destination doesn't bring a whole lot of interesting facts to the table – our respective journeys there and back most certainly do.

We all must temporarily induce a deep trance state of consciousness before entering or returning from the Free Dimension in a dream state. This means that we will find ourselves between dimensions and open to energy that may wish to communicate with us or try and adversely affect us.

As an experienced deep trance medium, I will effectively induce this state of consciousness so that spirit guides from the Free Dimension can connect with me. This allows me to mediate communication between my guides and members of my group from the physical world. This is also how I manage to write my books, give or take the odd bit of editing here and there.

The point being that whilst in this state of consciousness it is possible for any one of us to interact with souls from the Free Dimension in not only a telepathic mode – but also by physical means.

Most people, who claim they have seen a ghost, often state that they suddenly woke up and the image of a person was standing at the end of their bed staring back at them. Think back to when my wife saw my "attacker" beside my bed, then think back even further to my Native American spirit guide sitting at the bottom of my bed. In nearly all of these cases you will find that only a split second after witnessing a ghost, it will suddenly disappear as your full consciousness is resumed and all ties are cut to the Free Dimension. This is because our deep trance state is normally bypassed extremely quickly between both dimensions. However, if something is continually on our mind; something that can't be easily addressed, then it becomes more common to regularly find yourself aware of this place where virtually anything goes.

This is the only place where nightmares can occur, not in the dream state - as Freud naively believed. My own recurrent nightmare at the hands of my Jacobean "killer" always took place in this state of mind. The reason for this, as I'm sure you have worked out by now, is that the place between worlds is where you travel to if you are stuck in an interdimensional loop.

Of course, many of our nightmares are not directly as a result of any loop. Sometimes things happen in our present physical life that just cannot be digested easily. People suffering from PTSD or people who have been victims of abuse will regularly find themselves in a deep trance state and find it extremely difficult to break free from the excruciating emotions associated with the past events. It is highly likely that if these debilitating emotions are not suitably dealt with in a positive fashion then a loop will ensue after passing over. However, every case is different and it really depends on the particular circumstances and also the behaviour of the people involved.

I am often asked which of the spiritual guidelines is the most difficult to master when attempting to obtain your spiritual passport. My guides are always unanimous in declaring that it is overcoming the adverse effects of materialism. Materialism is the 'Hillary Step' that everyone fears before eventually reaching the summit. In my own case, I know that I murdered a member of my family in order to extract individual power and wealth within the Jacobean period. In a future life in Australia, I did not commit murder for those precise reasons. Analysing life in this way highlights a major difference but this will only become more transparent to us once we reach the Free Dimension where every soul thrives on their ability to integrate seamlessly.

We may only ever be a small part of the evolution of eternal life but we will have the opportunity to join the most wonderful collective imaginable. I can promise you that every loop that you have to withstand will be worth every ounce of hardship and toil that you endure before you can reach your very own Wailua Falls – a place where opulence and magnificence reside in abundance.

Your destiny now awaits you.

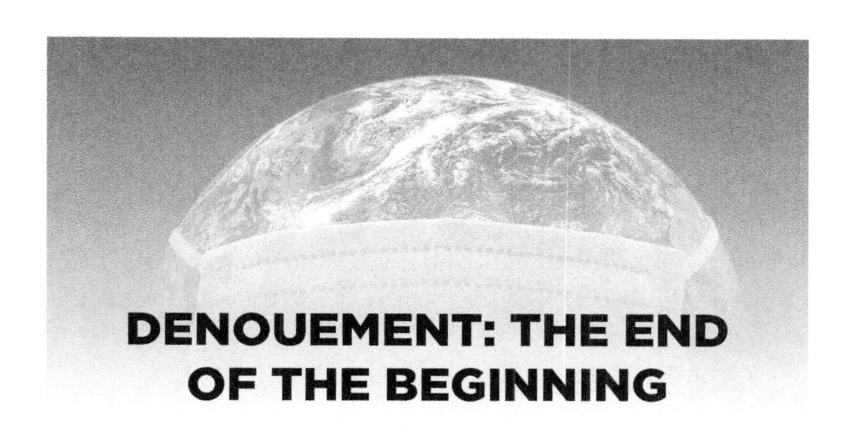

DENOUEMENT: THE END OF THE BEGINNING

As I once again find myself standing on the rooftop of the high-rise building in Irvine, Ayrshire – a mere five years after initially looking down upon the glory of all human life in the many forms that it presents, I am now left precariously pondering the future of all mankind. This now dilapidated building is soon to be demolished as the residents have chosen to escape the relative security of a huge built up concrete mass in favour of smaller individual dwellings that discretely hide behind increasingly deserted streets.

In the time that it has taken me to write this book, a horrific fire in a London tower block has cost the lives of many souls due to the wilful neglect of the landlord. An inevitable fear that this immense human tragedy may strike again has enforced all buildings of a similar structure to be condemned as they're now considered to be dangerous to society, resulting in the usual widespread panic measures throughout each and every local authority group.

More recently, as global societies began to protect themselves from imminent danger in so many other fields of conflict – a dark and mysterious cloud has slowly approached from the East, which to this date has refused to go away.

What follows is an in-depth account of my life experiences during the tumultuous events of the year 2020 and how the impact of everything since will affect the world as we effectively know it.

JANUARY 2020 – A NEW YEAR AND A NEW MESSAGE

January is that traditional time of the year when many of us decide to make a commitment to either ourselves or our respective communities, with a reflective view to improving life as we generally understand it. The opportunity to reflect on many missed opportunities of the year just past often allows us the luxury of preparing a more salubrious path to follow in the forthcoming twelve months.

As an established firm believer in life after death, my own personal ambitions are never really that prominent in my thoughts during this time. After all, I have been taught by my spiritual elders that 'time' is only ever an issue in a perennially decaying society, so the herald of a brand new yearly cycle should only ever be viewed as a celebratory tradition in my book. Yet, since initially writing about my journey through life over seven years ago, I've been sitting gingerly on tender hooks at the beginning of each calendar year, tentatively awaiting notification from my spirit team that something sinister was going to arrive on our doorstep.

Back in 2013, I can vividly remember being informed that I was to be ready for a major event that would change the lives of every single person in this world, and that all my spiritual endeavours – whether it be through writing, teaching, meditating or healing – were all just tools to be readied in preparation for whatever was to come. But... it never came. Every year I prepared for battle but the war never arrived. Not that I was disappointed, as I knew deep down that whatever was coming would be hugely challenging, but what exactly, and when?

The only clue I was ever given was that society would rebel against authority, resulting in widespread civil unrest. This would initially begin in the United States before spreading to all parts of the world. I was informed that countries wouldn't necessarily rage war against each other, but rather internal warfare would be at the forefront, and it would be extensive. The cause of this conflict was never revealed to me.

So, with the exact same expectations as every other year, I met up with the members of my trance mediumship group in Prestwick, Ayrshire, at the beginning of January. This small group consists of experienced local mediums and spiritual healers who all wish to explore the virtues of deep trance mediumship and meditation. I have been teaching this group for several years and they have all developed the ability to channel spirit people through their mediumship so that we can receive knowledge that will enable us to help us better understand life in all formats.

As a teaching group, it is important that all students are given as much practice as possible in the art of attaining a profound state of deep trance. However, just after arriving at the venue, I was advised by my guides to prepare myself for trance rather than the students. I immediately knew at this point that there was something very important that they wished to express to the group.

As a rule, I am not usually that aware of what is channelled direct from spirit when I am in a deep trance state. The group members will normally inform me of what has been said once I return to full consciousness. Additionally, I usually communicate with my guides once I return to my home, just in case I have failed to pick up on everything that was brought forward at the meeting. However, at this meeting in January, I was surprisingly aware of most of what was being said during my trance state. My guide, Mr Chung, informed the group that everyone was to be prepared for a huge shift in energy in the coming year. He added that our world would never quite be the same again after the forthcoming events of 2020.

Afterwards, I discussed Chung's revelation with the group members and we tried to fathom just what this meant for all of us. I knew that Mr Chung was not in the habit of making predictions so there was no way of finding out from him exactly what was about to happen. All we could do was speculate... and be ready!

Deep down, I still felt that the issue would be widespread civil unrest, yet there was no evidence of anything about to transpire in the world at that time. In fact, the only current affair dominating our news headlines was a little known virus that had affected a few unfortunate souls in China, but at the start of January nobody in their right mind ever suspected that this would deeply affect anyone in the UK, never mind the whole world.

Nevertheless, everyone in our group knew that something extremely worrying would soon arrive on our doorstep and if Chung was advising us to be prepared, then it would happen very soon.

FEBRUARY 2020 - CONFIRMATION

By the beginning of February it was confirmed that several cases of a type of Coronavirus, later to be called Covid-19, had spread to mainland Italy from China. This new virus had now been responsible for many hundreds of deaths in China and other countries in South East Asia, and the World Health Organisation quickly declared the Coronavirus a public health emergency of international concern. Here in the UK, we didn't seem too worried, and in all honesty I still did not think that this virus was the big dark cloud that Mr Chung had warned us about. That is, until another deep trance session took place in the middle of February.

There are several mediumship development groups within my local area and I will regularly organise trance workshops with the mediums that run them. During one of these workshops I was informed by a spirit guide being channelled through another trance medium that the Coronavirus would become a huge pandemic. When

I asked the guide if the virus was detrimental to our long term future on this planet I was informed that the virus was unfortunately a necessary evil. The guide added that there were too many people living on Earth with not enough food to feed them, and we should therefore try to refrain from eating animals.

This was a powerful message sent from a highly evolved guide working through a very experienced trance medium. It was a message that made me sit up and take notice; further giving me confirmation that what Chung had predicted was about to happen.

When I communicated with my guides after that workshop I was furnished with information that shook me to the core. The incoming virus would be devastating for the world as a health issue – but the shockwaves afterwards would be the real concern – both socially and economically. In other words, the repercussions from this pandemic would create civil disruption due to widespread financial and public-liberty restrictions.

MARCH 2020 - CORONAVIRUS ARRIVES IN THE UK

In March 2020, the World Health Organisation publicly declared COVID-19 a pandemic. They also expressed deep concern over alarming levels of inaction in many countries who refused to acknowledge the severity of what they were about to face. Finally, after huge public pressure, President Trump announced a national emergency in the United States and unlocked billions of dollars in funding to fight the spread of the disease. Suddenly, the world took notice – and held its breath.

The UK Government then followed suit by deciding to enforce the power to restrict public gatherings. All major sports and recreational events were temporarily halted – until this virus could be kept under control. On the 23rd of March, Prime Minister Boris Johnston announced on television that the people of the United

Kingdom should now stay at home to fight the spread of the Coronavirus, whilst the Treasury would foot the bill for lost income. This was a significant step to take and 'Official Lockdown' had begun in earnest.

The reality was that people of all ages were now dying from the debilitating effects of this virus and the emergency services of all countries braced themselves for the worst public health crisis in more than a hundred years.

Like most people, I thought that lockdown would consist of just two or three weeks of staying indoors until the threat of the virus had eased significantly to allow 'normality' to return. After all, wasn't the Coronavirus just a minor respiratory illness that only really affected the elderly or individuals suffering from other chronic conditions? I suppose the answer to this question rather depended on which form of media outlet you chose to give your time to, as all of a sudden experts in the field of 'unknown killer virus' began to spring up from every nook and cranny that forever held a grudge against society. As a result, widespread paranoia at this time almost became a bigger problem than the actual virus itself.

Suddenly we all had far too much time on our hands, much of which was spent listening to Government experts on national television giving their view on the severity of our predicament. By the end of March, the true horror of what we were all about to face was evident to see in hospitals all over Italy and Spain. Young and old were virtually fighting for their lives in hospital corridors and overworked medical staff could not cope.

In Scotland, the general consensus was that we should be safe from the virus. There were only a few sporadic cases confirmed and public health authorities seemed to have rammed home the message to all and sundry that the virus could be contained by good hygienic practices. We waited… and we waited… and we waited, until the infection rate rapidly increased. We braced ourselves for the inevitable.

APRIL 2020 – A TIME FOR ANSWERS

Lockdown remained in place going into April as the death rate all over Europe rapidly increased. Yet, despite all the misery and heartache caused by the killer virus, a new wave of optimism started to rise up from the shadow of death that stalked our hospitals in the UK. Yes, people were still dying alone in horrible conditions, but for those who were left on the front line to help care for the afflicted, a hero-like respect quickly grew legs, lifting public spirits in a way that seemed highly unlikely in the previous month.

Thankfully, the media paranoia that had dampened the mood of a nation in March had suddenly been transformed into a post-Dunkirk, stiff upper lip, two-fingered defiance that almost catapulted emergency staff into idolised warriors in the fight against COVID-19. Every Thursday evening, those of us interned by the lockdown, stood on our doorsteps and applauded the work of the British emergency services. This was a show of respectful support that spread nationally and even interrupted the evening viewing on national television.

As the public applauded the work of our medical heroes, hospital staff returned the gesture by standing outside of their workplaces and applauding the general public for their support. Before long, everyone stood outside of their homes every Thursday evening and nodded over appreciatively to our neighbours. We were all in this together and to win this war we needed the power of community spirit. Soon, many of our vulnerable citizens would struggle to feed themselves as the detrimental effects of the lockdown began to restrict the production and delivery of essential items.

Many people decided to help those affected in this way – and a new breed of hero was born. Society was being throttled by a killer determined to destroy our way of life, but the human spirit was not going to give up so easily. In many ways, this virus was in fact bringing people together, instead of isolating them. Suddenly... there was hope.

By the middle of April, I decided that I now needed some answers from my spirit friends. In my mind I knew that the only real way of achieving this was through the means of deep trance mediumship – and it needed to be performed by myself.

But, there was one small problem. I needed someone to ask questions and then take note of the answers given by my spirit guides. I couldn't ask any of my trance group as lockdown restrictions meant that nobody could visit any other household at this time. Nor could I instigate an online demonstration as my guides would never approve of this form of communication. So, during a meditation I asked my guides for advice and they intimated that my son, Dylan, was ready and capable of assisting me. Although Dylan is a very mature young man, he is only fifteen years old and I had reservations about involving anyone under eighteen. However, if my guides assured me that Dylan was ready and capable of assisting me then I at least had a guarantee that everything should go smoothly, so I discussed everything with Dylan and we both decided that on the 17th of April we would attempt to communicate with my trance team.

Dylan was naturally a little apprehensive at first, but he was also eager to find out more about the events of the upcoming months. I asked him to compile a list of questions that he thought would be relevant in terms of the way the world was shaping up for the coming year, and not to dwell too much on personal choices as spirit guides are reluctant to interfere with your chosen life path unless completely necessary.

Remarkably, Dylan seemed to take this all in his stride and I knew instantly that Chung had already started working with him subconsciously. Before I went into trance Dylan asked if he could video record the event on his phone. I said that he would need to ask my guides for their permission once they commenced communication with him.

We decided to use my home office to perform the trance mediumship and forty five minutes later I had regained full consciousness. Dylan said that he was a bit scared when a spirit person at first started to channel through me but that he soon got used to it and subsequently really enjoyed the experience. He added that Chung had given him permission to video the trance so we could now play back the recording and ponder the answers to Dylan's questions.

As the video recording began, I wasn't surprised to find that the images had darkened so that you couldn't see my face, just as my guides started to communicate. Thankfully though, they didn't affect the sound.

Dylan's questions and the answers given by my guides were as follows –

1. **When will the Covid 19 pandemic end?**
   The virus will be eradicated by the end of this calendar year.

2. **What will the total death-toll be?**
   There will be many thousands of deaths.

3. **How did it all start?**
   The virus was engineered by man.

4. **What can we do to prevent something like this happening in the future?**
   Learn lessons, be prepared, and stop eating animals.

5. **Will any of my family get the virus or be badly affected by it?**

None of your immediate family will be badly affected by this.

6. **Will the NHS in Scotland be able to cope with the effects of the virus?**
   In good time they will manage to cope with it.

7. **When will the lockdown end and when will be able to return to normal?**
   In your timeframe - by the end of June. However, this will not be the time for normality; it will only be a beginning.

Dylan then asked my guides other questions about his own spiritual journey and the answers to those questions shall remain private.

After the trance session, I asked my guides for more clarification on how the virus had originated. I was informed that although the virus was genetically engineered by man, it had never been intended to be spread amongst humans. It had been tested on animals and then spread to humans after being consumed - in other words – a tragic accident resulting from immoral practices.

I was further informed that we would all reap the benefits of lessons learned from the pandemic, but that it will take some considerable time before that happens. I will explain this in more detail during the final chapter of the book.

MAY 2020 – CIVIL UNREST BEGINS

By the beginning of May 2020 the people of the United Kingdom had been stuck in a Government imposed lockdown for nearly six weeks. In this time almost five percent of the population had been infected by the virus. This included Prime Minister, Boris Johnson, who spent several nights in the intensive care ward of a London hospital.

Despite the continuing high risk of extensive deaths due to complications arising from the virus, the Government knew that there would be huge detrimental financial implications to the economy if the lockdown continued for much longer. Stuck in the middle of a healthcare versus accountancy social sandwich, Boris Johnson promised that lockdown restrictions would begin to ease by the end of May if the rate of infection could be reduced to an acceptable standard. Thankfully it did and restrictions began to ease ever so slightly.

In truth, the country needed a light at the end of a very dark tunnel, and whilst the complete ending of lockdown restrictions still looked a long way off, this first step did give the public hope. Keeping public moral in a positive light was Boris Johnson's most difficult task during this period. Across the pond, in the good old US of A, President Trump faced a much bigger challenge as the month of May drew to a dramatic close.

On the 25th of May 2020, an online video recording of an African American male being slowly suffocated by a white Minneapolis Police Officer sent shockwaves throughout the civilised world. George Floyd had been arrested by three police officers and was forcibly being restrained by the knee of one of the officers as he lay on a public street. Mr Floyd appeared to be choking and saying that he was struggling to breathe but the officer continued to kneel on his neck until an ambulance arrived. He was pronounced dead shortly after arriving at hospital.

On the 26th day of May, protests began on the streets of Minneapolis in response to the unlawful killing of an African American man by a white police officer. Soon, the protests would spread nationwide before eventually reaching over two thousand cities and towns in over sixty countries of the world.

The effects of a killer virus were suddenly forgotten as news reports suggested a new, more intense terror was lurking on every street corner.

JUNE 2020 – THE WORLD PROTESTS

In the first week of June, there were widespread media reports of rioting and looting across the streets of almost all of America's major cities. Streets that only a few days ago were deserted due to the virus were now seemingly full of protestors marching shoulder to shoulder in solidarity against socio-economic inequality and discrimination.

At the heart of the protests was a social and political movement called 'Black Lives Matter', who were specifically protesting against any form of police brutality and racially motivated violence against black people.

President Trump now faced a new crisis in the wake of the US economy being hobbled by a deadly pandemic. His response was to deploy specially-trained riot police and also thousands of troops from the National Guard to try and restore order.

By the end of June, BLM protests had spread around the globe. Here, in the United Kingdom, protestors began tearing down statues of anyone who was associated with slavery in the nineteenth century.

As I watched the news coverage of events as they happened, a chill ran down the back of my neck. For seven years I had waited for something like this to occur, knowing that the repercussions for society would be devastating. Now it was literally on my doorstep.

A few of my friends and colleagues began to ask me if I knew what the outcome would be, since my guides had previously predicted the civil unrest. I had to reply that I didn't know. In all honesty, I was petrified to try and find out. Yet for some unknown reason; a positive feeling remained in my mind, knowing that things always happen for a reason, no matter the circumstances or consequences. Perhaps, for all of us, I believed deep down that there was an important lesson in there, somewhere, somehow.

Public opinion was fairly divided in the United States. Most people were in agreement that equality is vitally important in a modern day society, but how could equality exist in a country where the wealth divide is astronomical? In layman's terms – it never could. Moreover, the long term fiscal damage from the Coronavirus would simply compound this perception.

Only a few weeks before, the world was gripped by a killer virus. It was all we ever spoke about or watched on news bulletins. The entire world was gripped by the uncertainty of something that we knew very little about. Now, as the month of June slowly dissipated into the periodic memoirs of overworked journalists, it seemed as if the virus had simply disappeared into insignificance. The media world now had a new toy to play with - and you could be sure they were going to get their money's worth.

JULY 2020 - VL DAY

The effects of a nationwide lockdown in the UK had reduced the number of new cases of Coronavirus significantly from its height in April. At the beginning of July there were almost ninety percent less people being admitted to hospital and the death rate had become extremely low.

Lockdown had already been eased from the beginning of May for certain shops and essential services, but it was the reopening of the hospitality sector on the 4th of July that really signalled a huge step towards the beginning of normality for the country as a whole.

Strict safety measures were put in place on a national level for all premises and adherence to these regulations were non-negotiable. However, it was a huge relief for everyone to finally be able to socialise in public for the first time in months. The light at the end of the tunnel now shone as brightly as the midday summer sun. Public moral was at a new high as everyone celebrated Victory over Lockdown.

On the other hand, experts now warned of a second wave of Covid-19 cases soon arriving due to restrictions being lifted. The battle may have been won but the war still raged on.

Elsewhere, protests against inequality continued in the Unites States and most of Western Europe. The monument of Confederate General Robert E. Lee was substantially vandalised on the 1st of July, and in London, the statue of Winston Churchill was defaced.

It was clear that intense animosity still circulated around the globe in many formats and guises. Social media video recordings simply increased these feelings of deep-rooted fury and resentment. Suddenly, media personalities were self-righteously educating us on the immoral practices of human slavery, whilst driving around in luxury sports cars that were manufactured by companies that once financially supported the Third Reich.

It was clear to see that human equality could never be achieved with so much political, societal and economical divide. The joy of being able to now meet up with friends over a nice meal or drink was a huge step in returning society to some form of familiarity; yet the turbulent debates of man's inhumane actions, whether in the past, present or future, remained in a melting pot of superfluous emotions, and it would take more than a killer virus to finally break this down.

AUGUST 2020 - CALM BEFORE THE STORM

All schools finally reopened in Scotland during August and this marked a significant change in direction for society. If we were prepared to let our children integrate with each other, no matter the guidelines introduced, then we had surely put a precedent in place that would enable us to look forward to a complete return to normality.

It seemed like we were now in control of the virus rather than the other way around – and it felt strangely comforting. Elsewhere, schools in England were due to return in September and it was hoped that the success of the reopening of public authority residences would then ensure that the UK as a whole could prepare for the eventual reopening of private establishments like cinemas, theatres, leisure centres and sports stadiums.

In many other European countries, the easing of lockdown restrictions was already a few weeks ahead of the UK. In almost all of them, a second major spike of

Covid-19 cases had occurred and caused authorities there to reintroduce further restrictions. Health experts in the UK predicted a similar occurrence would likely happen here. Our trust was firmly placed in the hands of the public and now we could only wait and see.

In the Unites States, BLM protests began to significantly ease towards the end of the month. The general public then started to realise that the media had drastically exaggerated the amount of violence that had taken place on American streets. It was true that many incidents had occurred between both protestors and anti-protestors, but statistics now revealed that over ninety percent of all public protests had passed by peacefully with no arrests.

To me, it came as no surprise that the easing of both lockdown restrictions and public protests occurred simultaneously. Whenever you restrict the movement of people then they will automatically rebel against any form of restraint, whether it is considered just or not. Any form of injustice then witnessed will almost certainly ignite emotions that are already simmering to the point of boiling over. The use of social media only exacerbates public emotions and feelings until you are instinctively urged to choose one side or the other.

The warm summer nights of August passed by as revellers finally enjoyed socialising in open air pubs and restaurants, which were eager to try and make up for months of lost revenue. But then again, the calm of the night often makes way for the eye of the storm…

SEPTEMBER 2020 – FACE TO FACE WITH COVID-19

The expected huge rise in Covid-19 cases arrived at the beginning of September, although most of the outbreaks were fairly localised, resulting in lockdown restrictions being reintroduced to just the areas affected. Nevertheless, it was clear that it was only a matter of time before more widespread constraints were put in place.

Public moral began to dip again and the media continued to focus on how badly the public had recently behaved rather than how many lives had been saved by sacrificing so many civil liberties over the course of the last six months.

By the middle of September, everything in my household seemed almost as normal as it had been before the virus outbreak. My family and I could more or less venture wherever we wanted to – both locally and nationally, knowing that extensive protection was in place in every establishment or humble abode that we chose to visit. So, when my son Dylan woke up one morning in the middle of September with a sore throat and a runny nose, we just presumed that he had caught a common cold and would be fine in a few days' time. Sure enough, three days later his throat was much better and he felt absolutely fine – except for being left with the remnants of a minor cough.

Dylan had no underlying symptoms of Covid-19. Even his cough did not seem to be too intrusive. However, my intuition kept telling me differently and I asked him if he was willing to go and get tested for the virus, mainly because his grandparents are elderly and vulnerable to this disease. Dylan decided not to get tested as he was sure he wasn't infected, but then again he did decide to stay indoors for the next few days just to be on the safe side.

Six days after Dylan first showed signs of a virus, Anne then presented a sore throat and runny nose, almost identical to the symptoms that Dylan had. Anne had been in the company of her elderly mother a few days previously so she decided to get tested just to be on the safe side. Who knows – maybe her intuition was also kicking in strongly as the next morning her test result came back. It was positive.

To say we were all shocked was an understatement. Both Dylan and I were then tested later that day. The next morning the results both came back as negative.

A local Health Board employee telephoned Anne and issued guidelines on how long we would all have to self-isolate and furthermore - how best to stay apart in our household to avoid infecting each other.

For the next fortnight we all tried our best to avoid each other but it became almost impossible. In all honesty, you would have to live inside a spacesuit to have any chance of escaping this highly contagious virus from within a family home. Even so, I did not display symptoms of any virus during this time, nor did Dylan. We tried to work out where the virus came from and why only Anne tested positive, but we couldn't come up with a definite answer.

On reflection, it was clear that Dylan and Anne had the exact same symptoms, yet only Anne tested positive. Could it be that Dylan tested negative as the virus had already left his body? As for me, the only explanation that I could give for not catching the virus was that I suffered from a common cold in December of last year that had very similar symptoms and which lasted for over a fortnight. Could that virus have been Covid-19 - even that far back?

We all self-isolated as requested and both Anne and Dylan made a full recovery. It had been a frightening period for my family but the virus's bark had clearly been much worse than its bite. We had undoubtedly been very fortunate.

Dylan believed that he may have caught the virus from a student at his school. Ironically, the student only showed symptoms of a common cold and not Coronavirus and had therefore attended school as regulations imply.

By the end of September, the UK Government and all the devolved local Parliaments, came together to initiate tighter and stricter public regulations to try and stem the tide of positive cases of the virus. They warned that if infection rates did not decrease dramatically in the next few weeks then a second full lockdown was inevitable.

As I sat at home listening to political leaders and health experts give their views on how to best safeguard the public, I wondered just how many people were attending schools, visiting grandparents, shopping in supermarkets, working in front-line services or even just meeting up with friends to discuss the perils of the world – and not knowing that the common cold that they were presently suffering from could in fact be a killer virus.

The light at the end of that tunnel had started to dim again. As the colder and darker nights now approached, it was clearly now a time for the world's Governments to make some difficult and unpopular decisions – or major civil unrest would inevitably return with a vengeance.

OCTOBER 2020 – WHEN HISTORY IS MADE

The date is now Thursday the 24th September 2020; exactly one week away from the beginning of October, so in essence I am now writing about the future.

A wise old man once told me that whenever I sigh despondently or curse obtusely at whatever happens to be obstructing my chain of thoughts, a tiny butterfly that's invisible to the human eye, flutters off to a place of relative safety, in the hope of finding the voices of reason. These voices listen carefully to the sound of the little butterfly, before advising on the path that it then must take. Should it fly back to where it first came from, or just remain in solitude until its tender wings can flap no more?

Every little butterfly that flies off to the Free Dimension takes a small piece of us with it. Think of it as a Post-It Note being delivered back to your guides, advising them of your welfare. Every Post-It Note is then carefully studied and acted upon by our guides. The note becomes the cause and the action becomes the effect – karma is thus created.

A wise old man recently told me that millions upon millions of little butterflies were currently fluttering in solitude, patiently waiting till the time is right in order to return to their original source, and thus deliver the effect. Whatever this effect transpires to be will in due course transform the lives of every one of us.

This process will commence near the end of October 2020 and the repercussions shall be felt before the end of the calendar year. If you are reading this - then you may already know in what direction we are now heading.

There is a strange weather phenomenon, named St Elmo's fire, where luminous blue plasma balls of light appear during electrical storms. In 1899, the inventor of the first alternating current electricity supply system, Nikola Tesla, created St Elmo's fire in his laboratory whilst testing his innovative Tesla coil transformer circuit. He was later reported to have said that the blue plasma that was created lit up the wings of butterflies as they flew around the room.

For every storm that is created, St Elmo's fire shows us that there is still beauty in everything that surrounds us, no matter the havoc that is created or the rage bestowed upon us. Peace shall always follow any storm, just like the calm that preceded it.

A wise old man once told me that in the not too distant future all of our little butterflies will once again fly off to the Free Dimension with messages of hope and compassion. When they return to us we will have found our path.

Today is Thursday the 24th of September. Very soon you will begin to write your own history. Namaste.

2020 THE END OF THE BEGINNING

Imagine, if you will, that you are sitting at home on a wet, Monday morning, just staring blankly at four white walls. Your partner has already left for work and has left a list of jobs for you to attend to, since you don't have to go to work today, tomorrow or any other day for that matter.

Your children are continually running past your feet in a mad rush to get ready for school, despite only being half-dressed and still to consume their hastily prepared breakfast. The dog's nose repeatedly nudges your knee in a desperate attempt to entice you to take him for a walk, whilst the commencement of the washing machine's final spin abruptly reminds you that last night's clothes are almost ready for the dryer.

You continue staring at the four white walls and they begin to feel like a prison cell as you ponder if this is what life is really meant to be like. Suddenly, an unusual sound breaks the monotony and you immediately come to your senses. The doorbell doesn't usually ring this early in the morning so you quickly arise from your battle-hardened armchair and discover a friendly face at your doorstep. Your neighbour has decided to pay you a visit in a bid to try and cheer you up.

As you both sit on opposite armchairs, whilst the morning chaos continues to bombard the ambience of the sitting room, your neighbour decides to offer you a wonder drug. He hands it over to you and states that you only need to take one sniff from this magical drug and all your troubles will disappear. He adds that this special potion has no detrimental health effects and can make life seem wonderful again.

You are apprehensive at first, but decide to try the drug just this one time. Suddenly, you are aware of your mind leaving your body behind as it floats around the room effortlessly. You notice that the television is switched on and you can see that it's playing the greatest movie of all time. You then hear the most beautiful song ever written being played on the stereo. Incredibly, you notice that the stale smell of tobacco has now left the room to be replaced by the smell of freshly baked bread in the morning. Not only can you smell the freshness of the bread but you can now almost taste it – garnished with rich dairy butter and homemade strawberry jam.

"Wake up dad!" shouts your daughter.

"I need you to drive me to school or I will be late."

You quickly realise that you have fallen asleep and there is no friendly neighbour with a wonder drug. It has all been a dream – albeit a very pleasant one.

After the kids have left for school, the dog walked and the dirty clothes all washed, dried and ironed, you have the chance to sit back down and face those infamous four white walls. You think about that surreal moment when all of reality suddenly became irrelevant and trouble-free. You wonder what life would be like if you could just take that one sniff of a wonder drug and sail off to a land where only you mattered – where it was only you who would decide how life treated you, and where the responsibility for any of your actions always lay elsewhere. Then, you realise – it means absolutely nothing without purpose.

On reflection – you didn't decide to go back to sleep and to the perfect dream – you chose to take responsibility for your life, and help to improve the lives of the people you care about. Life in a dream-world where the fruits of labour are all self-centred cannot feasibly exist when you leave unfinished business behind. You will naturally look back with regret and try everything in your power to rectify your actions.

That perfect moment, when all thoughts are wondrously free and sensuously pure, really and truly does exist. One day, every one of us will return to the place where dreams are made of. You will watch the most wonderful movies and listen to the most beautiful music that you can ever imagine. I can promise you that this is a place where you will want to remain forever and never wish to leave. Unless, you leave behind unfinished business.

It is imperative that our life in the physical world allows us to achieve all the goals that we initially set. No stone can ever be left unturned as the weight of being pulled back to Earth by a heavily-burdened conscience will create an interdimensional loop that we now know is extremely difficult to break free from.

It really doesn't matter if you need to return to Earth because you never spent enough time with your family, or because you callously murdered people in Australia, as your conscience mind belongs to you and you only. Remember that you are the sole judge and jury – it is your own standards that must be adhered to at all times, and nobody else's.

Every time a little butterfly returns to the Free Dimension it leaves behind a small legacy with those who choose to look out for us. They are only ever there to advise us. You will always have the final say on every thought or action that crosses your mind. Your legacy is only ever there to remind you of yourself.

As is on Earth, the Free Dimension is not populated by perfect souls – only knowledgeable souls. We continue to learn from others and from ourselves. This is what eternal life constitutes as it continually evolves day by day, thought by thought. Your involvement in this process is forever justifiable.

The presence of interdimensional loops within our eternal lives is massively important to not only our own personal development but also that of the world as a whole. We have now discovered that by returning to the 'scene of the crime', that we can begin to re-evaluate past thoughts or actions in a bid to become more self-aware of how karma is essential to an evolving soul. Only then can negative emotions and prejudices be transformed into luminous blue plasma balls of light that surround the wings of our beloved butterflies.

Our world, as we know it, now finds itself in the midst of an enormous interdimensional loop. Hugely disconcerting events from our past that should have educated us greatly on the power of love over conflict have slowly started to cast a dangerous shadow over the whole of humanity.

Almost one hundred years ago, a virus killed fifty million people throughout the world. It lasted for over two years and in that time claimed more lives than World War 1. It is estimated that one third of the world's population became infected by this devastating strain of influenza.

Almost one hundred years ago, a catastrophic economic depression began in the United States, which quickly spread throughout the rest of the world. The world's economies had still not recovered when ten years later - World War 2 commenced. Now, as the harrowing effects of the Covid-19 epidemic starts to sink its teeth into the hearts of our global economic infrastructures, it is vital that we don't repeat the mistakes of almost a century ago.

Materialism, as we now know is only a stimulant designed to test our resolve. Yet, once bitten by a desire to reach the height of opulence in an increasingly shallow society, many souls will become fearful of losing sight where vision should be clear and precise.

Almost one hundred years ago, a young physicist by the name of Theodor Kaluza, presented a hypothesis to Albert Einstein that extended his theory of general relativity into a fifth dimensional capability. Subsequent interpretations of this discovery diluted the theory into what we now have today – the theory of quantum gravity. The mechanics of this theory have been interpreted by some of the greatest physicists who have ever lived and countless incredible scientific feats have subsequently been achieved in many fields. Nevertheless, if the Fifth dimension is in fact the Free Dimension as we have been advised by the writers of this book, then we have to ask ourselves if we have really even scratched the surface of this incredible discovery, since we are no further forward in finding intelligent communication from outside of our planet's orbit.

When I look back at the answers given by my spirit guide during the trance session with my son in April, there are a few that stick in my mind.

The first one is the response to whether any of Dylan's immediate family would get the virus or be badly affected by it. The guide only stated that none of Dylan's immediate family would be badly affected by the virus. On reflection, you could argue that he is implying that we would catch the virus, though we shouldn't worry too much about the consequences – which is exactly what transpired.

The second answer concerned the prediction that the virus would be eradicated at the end of the calendar year. Currently, our world is still caught in the grip of the worst of this virus and it is widely predicted by health experts that it will be with us till at least the middle of 2021, so it does seem highly unlikely that it will be gone by the end of the year. Still, the guide did predict the beginning of the end of the lockdown would be at the end of June – and this was spot on.

The third, and most potentially worrying answer, is the reply to the question on what we could do to prevent the virus from returning in the future. The guide stated that we should learn lessons and be better prepared, and as we discussed earlier – he confirmed that this will eventually come to fruition.

Initially, I felt that this was a reference to simply being better prepared for the imminent threat of a virus and having better public protection measures in place, but when I began writing this chapter I was informed of a much more sinister nature to the message. He was in fact suggesting that we should all have seen this coming many years ago, since humanity has not learned from its many lessons in history. Indeed, he was now implying that the world in general was about to revisit an interdimensional loop – in order to view the points in history when society began to capitulate almost one hundred years ago.

One hundred years ago, it was feared that the great flu epidemic would end humanity; such was the devastation that it brought. Nevertheless, humanity survived and subsequently built strong foundations for a full recovery. We must now ensure that strong foundations are once again laid in our lands when the present Coronavirus leaves our planet.

Almost one hundred years ago, a great economic depression brought widespread misery and suffering to millions of lives across our globe. We must now ensure that when the worst of the impending financial crisis arrives that we all fight it with the virtues of the ten spiritual guidelines behind us, rather than the utterly appalling values that once surfaced before.

Almost one hundred years ago, an amazing scientific breakthrough occurred when a scientist broke down the physical restraints of true consciousness and discovered the key elements of eternal life. One day, in the near but distant future, scientists will discover consciousness in the Fifth Dimension that possesses the ability to communicate with us in the physical world. The dawning of the Free Dimension will change the way we view life, view each other, and view ourselves. Many loops will be subsequently broken.

A wise old man once told me the story of a little butterfly that tried to return to the voices of reason in order to deliver a little Post It Note of hope. Unfortunately, something went drastically wrong and the little butterfly then found itself stuck in the middle of an interdimensional loop.

The butterfly was young and inexperienced and didn't realise that it just needed to stop for a moment and relax, thus letting the loop pass by without a glitch. Alas, the little butterfly panicked and began to flutter its wings as swiftly as it possibly could, hoping to break free from the restraints of the loop, but the more it flapped its wings the deeper and deeper it fell into the loop's enticing energy.

At that moment, out of the corner of one eye, the little butterfly could clearly see the people back on Earth running amok, tearing down buildings and setting fire to landscapes. The chaotic scenes caused the butterfly to flap its wings even faster, and as it did so - the chaos appeared to escalate even more back on Earth.

Out of the corner of its other eye, the butterfly could see a digital clock with the time and date displayed in a numerical format. All the numbers on the clock then started to vary as the butterfly's wings sped up, the minutes of time increasing rapidly as the date slowly began to decrease. This odd timeframe confused the little butterfly even further until its wings suddenly stopped flapping due to sheer and utter exhaustion.

The little butterfly then found itself floating all alone in a flightless environment until suddenly it could hear the most wonderful medley of songs emanating in the distance. As the butterfly automatically floated upwards towards the soft, melodic sound, its wings began to open up gently and it found it could flutter softly towards the direction of the soothing music.

Reaching its destination, the butterfly then conveyed the important communication that had taken so long to be delivered. The voices of reason then sent the little butterfly back home with an important message for mankind.

As the little butterfly began his journey home to the physical world, he became aware of millions upon millions of other butterflies fluttering closely behind, as if they had been waiting patiently on his arrival.

A wise old man informed me that this little butterfly had still not returned home to deliver the important message. It is also unclear at this stage just who will receive the important communication, but the recipient will feature strongly in the future shaping of our physical world.

Perhaps the recipient will be a young scientist with a fresh view on interdimensional life. It may even be a modern day Ghandi or Martin Luther King – ready to remind us how we should all utilise the art of protest as a form of reasoning as opposed to a lethal weapon. Or, perhaps, the recipient is you – the reader of this book, having been drawn to these words from a force greater than just personal choice.

Whoever the recipient may be, a huge task surely lies ahead for this individual to lead humanity in a new direction. Nevertheless, this can, and will be achieved, of that there is no doubt.

It is widely believed in the physical world that one solitary little butterfly can cause chaos throughout our planet by just flying against the wind. The reality is that this same butterfly can then bring balance to our world by permitting us to bring it home, thus triggering the end of the beginning…

I'm not going to lie to you. Our world is about to embark on a very difficult and dangerous voyage. The effects of the pandemic are still to really hit home and the welfare of the world's citizen's is literary hanging by a very thin thread. Sadly, there are no words in this book that can offer a quick fix to the many problems that we are all about to face. All I can say is that by following the intrinsic values that my guides have brought forward, you will stand in good stead when those spiritual passports are about to be authenticated, regardless of what is thrown at you in the coming months.

It is clear that the physical world is undoubtedly entering an interdimensional loop. There is nothing that you or I can now do to prevent this from occurring – sadly it's an inevitable consequence of society's overall refusal to learn from its lessons.

From our perspective – this is a hugely worrying period when the vast majority of souls will find themselves completely out of their comfort zone in a constant conflict, forever trying to preserve their status in a crumbling society. Yet, from the perspective of the

Free Dimension – this situation presents a monumental opportunity for millions of souls to revisit old haunts and finally break free from their restrictive loops.

The first forty years of the twentieth century on Earth heralded a stage of perilous living that caused millions of souls to perish at the hands of both callousness and extreme hardship. During this time period many souls committed acts upon others that would naturally be considered extremely difficult to condone when self-evaluation later commenced in the Free Dimension. Countless loops were inevitably created by the horrifying events that took place. You would have to imagine that if a subsequent opportunity then presented itself to return to a similar situation back on this physical plane, then most souls would eagerly accept the challenge. Sometimes acts of cruelty can be so severe that the only way to fully redeem your soul is to put yourself back into similar circumstances to see if you react differently this time.

Whatever lies ahead for us all will give these souls this vital opportunity to finally authenticate their spiritual passport. Many souls have returned to this world in preparation for this precise moment and it is for this reason that the ascended masters in the Free Dimension must endorse the predicament that we all now must face, however heartless that may appear to be to those among us who choose to believe that life is not eternal.

In the Free Dimension, the upcoming events are being looked upon as a welcome challenge that we should all embrace. The reality is that the greater prize awaits us all in the next dimension where all the troubles that we are about to endure do not exist, provided we can free ourselves from any troublesome loop. In other words – embrace whatever is thrown at you and come out of the other side smiling. It is a tall order but through hardship you will always find heroes; through conflict you will always find healers, and through destitution you will always find fortune – in our hearts if not in our stature.

We must forever understand that the imperfect soul is forever blessed with imperfections; the forgiving soul should forgive and not forget; the emotional soul should weep with the sting of sorrow; the knowledgeable soul should ignore fool's gold; the loving soul should love like there is no tomorrow; the truthful soul should feel the truth when declaring it; the successful soul should feel fulfilled with every failure; the humble soul should be proud of their modesty; the healing soul should be thankful of the trust bestowed upon them, and the eternal soul should be blessed with the opportunity to dance with the stars in the never-ending moonlight.

My final few paragraphs must come from the heart as I end my fourth and final book. It has been a privilege writing for you and in particular those readers who have supported all four books through thick and thin. I promised myself early on that I wouldn't write words that just made you feel good about yourself as there is no point in me wrapping you up in cotton wool when the big, bad wolf can easily blow you out the door. I will always be truthful and down to Earth – that is the only way that my guides can ever communicate with me. I believe that you deserve the truth in relative terms and that is why every word that I write has, at times, been an absolute prisoner. I can never afford to get something wrong, even though I regularly do, before being corrected in my dreams. Even now, I still doubt my ability to convey their messages, but I never doubt their abilities. Only last night, I felt that I should remove the section from the book that conveyed the declaration of the virus being completely gone by the end of 2020. I was quickly instructed that it should stay in place as there is a hidden meaning to this message that will only become apparent when the time is right.

So, after almost ten months of writing, I'm finally looking forward to a welcome period of recovery for my poor body. Every pound of my flesh has constantly ached for the last three hundred days due to not being able to sleep properly – that is the price you pay for working closely with the spirit world, sorry Free Dimension! But, you know what – it has been truly worth it. I have found the source of my loop and this can now be fully addressed when I eventually return home. Having said all that, this book must not be about me – for so many reasons it has to be about all of you.

Five years have passed since I initially started writing about the archetypes of eternal living and much of what surrounds our life on Earth has changed significantly in that time period. Having said that, the philosophy brought forward from the ascended masters of the Free Dimension hasn't altered at all. It is only our self-discovery and self-awareness that continually alters as we find better ways to seek internal peace.

It is therefore vitally important that you never forget the guidance brought forward in this book as you now enter a more challenging period of physical existence, and please, please, please remember to be kind to your neighbour when things get rough. I beg of you to respect every living creature that surrounds us regardless of the choices that they make. Others will eventually have the opportunity to judge their own actions, not you. Only your own choices or actions are important, no matter where you find yourself and in what capacity.

This world will perpetually survive, whether we have to return to the great intrinsic ways of the indigenous tribes or progress through innovative artificial intelligence. You will also survive – your life cannot end, it will always remain an important part of the great cycle. The light at the end of the tunnel shall never completely go out. Then, when the Free Dimension beckons, the tunnel will illuminate in a way that you never thought possible, making you feel more alive than you have ever felt.

The evolution of eternal life consumes us in the same way that a mother cradles her new-born. Finding ourselves at the cusp of Wailua Falls, preparing for a journey home on our big, red bus, we simply flutter our wings to the sound of church bells, heralding the birth of endless days and endless nights.

From this life to your life... a heartfelt thanks.

As always, I will leave the last word to my spirit friends; if you don't want to know the score... then look away now.

"In not less than two and no more than three thousand sundown's, the Earth will once again begin to breathe a little easier, as peace descends amongst its tribes. The winds of change shall soften until the gentle breeze of springtime arrives with a flurry of convalescence. The wages of sinful greed will have long perished in the deep sands of time, bringing resplendence to a world that was found lacking in morality. Laid bare amongst the unvirtuous hordes of vultures awaiting the beginning of the end, the spirit of humanity will rise up in stature and triumph, before gracefully announcing that it is just the end of the beginning..."

In memory of my mum and dad…
rest in peace.